In the **PATH** *of an* **AVALANCHE**

A TRUE STORY

In the **PATH**

of an AVALANCHE

VIVIEN BOWERS

GREYSTONE BOOKS
Douglas & McIntyre Publishing Group
Vancouver / Toronto / Berkeley

This book is dedicated to my mother, who also loves mountains.

V . B .

Greystone Books
A division of Douglas & McIntyre Ltd.
2323 Quebec Street, Suite 201
Vancouver, British Columbia
Canada V5T 4S7
www.greystonebooks.com

National Library of Canada Cataloguing in Publication Data
Bowers, Vivien, 1951
In the path of an avalanche : a true story / Vivien Bowers

ISBN 1-55054-518-3

1. Avalanches—Accidents—British Columbia—Selkirk Range.
2. Avalanches. I. Title.
QC929.A8B68 2003   551.57'848   C2003-910907-0

Library of Congress information is available upon request.

Editing by Barbara Pulling
Copy-editing by Elizabeth McLean
Cover and interior design by Jessica Sullivan
Cover photograph by © Galen Rowell/CORBIS
Map by Stuart Daniel
Printed and bound in Canada by Friesens
Printed on acid-free paper
Distributed in the U.S. by Publishers Group West

We gratefully acknowledge the financial support of the Canada Council for
the Arts, the British Columbia Arts Council, and the Government
of Canada through the Book Publishing Industry Development Program
(BDIDP) for our publishing activities.

In memory of those who lost their lives in
the January 2, 1998, avalanche
in Kokanee Glacier Provincial Park:

SCOTT MORGAN BRADLEY,
b. November 16, 1965

MARY ELIZABETH COWAN,
b. March 5, 1974

ROBERT MICHAEL PATRICK DRISCOLL,
b. March 17, 1962

GEOFFREY NORMAN LEIDAL,
b. October 5, 1966

LISE JEAN MARIE NICOLA,
b. August 13, 1968

GEORGE PATRICK VON BLUMEN,
b. May 9, 1965

{Contents}

✳

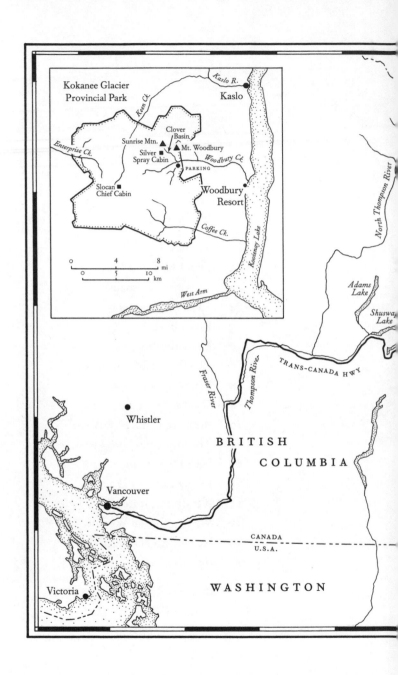

Kokanee Glacier
Provincial Park

Kaslo

Kaslo R.

Keen Ck.

Clover
Basin
Sunrise Mtn. ▲ ▲ Mt. Woodbury
Silver ■
Spray Cabin ●
Enterprise Ck.
● PARKING
Woodbury Ck.

Slocan ■
Chief Cabin

Woodbury
Resort

Coffee Ck.

Kootenay Lake

0   4   8
└─┴─┴─┴─┴─┴─┴─┴─┘ mi
0   5   10
└─┴─┴─┴─┴─┴─┘ km

West Arm

North Thompson River

Adams
Lake

Shuswap
Lake

Fraser River

Thompson River

TRANS-CANADA HWY

● Whistler

BRITISH

COLUMBIA

Vancouver
●

CANADA
- - -
U.S.A.

Victoria
●

WASHINGTON

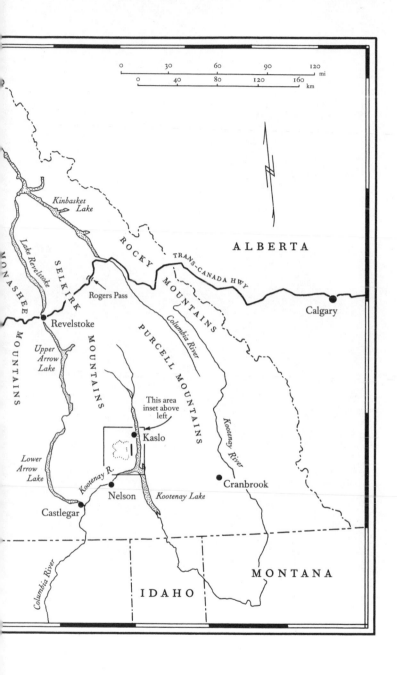

{Preface}

IN APRIL 1994, three friends and I flew by helicopter to the Silver Spray cabin in Kokanee Glacier Park, near where I live in southeastern British Columbia, for an Easter ski trip. Skiing back to the cabin late one afternoon, we crossed Clover Basin, a huge, open bowl where avalanches had obviously run in past years. Avoiding that slope would have meant backtracking, adding an extra couple of hours to the day. The quickest way "home" was across this south-facing bowl.

Spread well apart, the four of us dropped in turn onto a flatter bench to traverse the bowl. This wouldn't be the first time I had held my breath while skiing across a snow slope. I remember glancing up at the steep walls of the upper bowl above me, but mostly I concentrated on getting quickly to the other side. We crossed without incident, but I'll never know how safe that slope really was. The following day, on another south-facing slope, we set off a minor avalanche that took us for a short tumble, which tells you something about the snow stability at the time.

I frequently think about my traverse on that Easter afternoon. Every backcountry skier has taken calculated risks. I considered myself a cautious skier, and I figured I knew how to ski safely in avalanche terrain. But the slope I crossed was the site of a massive avalanche four years later. After writing about that event, I have come to suspect I was far too nonchalant.

Like many living in the area, I was hugely affected by the January 2, 1998, tragedy, which I first heard about on my car radio as I was driving to meet friends for a day in the backcountry. The event also raised some troubling questions for me. How could such an experienced group of skiers have been caught in a deadly slide? In the years that followed, I decided that the accident might serve as a powerful tool for exploring not only the hows and whys of this natural phenomenon but how it is that people find themselves in the path of an avalanche. It was something I, personally, needed to understand.

This was a difficult book to write, and I often felt as though I were walking a very fine line. I wanted readers to understand and learn from the events surrounding this avalanche, yet I did not want to exploit the tragedy, cast blame, or cause further distress to families and friends still struggling to move on with their lives. The writer in me knew that I had to "bring to life" people involved in the tragedy to illustrate how devastating an avalanche can be and to make this a compelling narrative. At the same time, I sympathized with those who weren't interested in becoming characters in a book or were concerned about sensationalism. In the end, I was moved by the willingness of many of those I contacted to trust me with their experiences and memories. A few people thanked me for the opportunity to talk about the accident or about their absent friends for the first time in years. Some were trembling as they recounted events, but they felt it was important to do so. Others, however, were upset that I was focusing on such a personal tragedy and asked me to reconsider. As a writer, I am always making use of the experiences of others, but it's an aspect of my work I wrestle with, and never more so than when working on this project.

Because I was seeking information about an event that had taken place several years before, many of my interviewees were vague on details, and there were many discrepancies among accounts. I've done my best to piece together what happened, but those who were present at the time will undoubtedly question particular details. I decided at the outset that I would not fictionalize any aspects of the event, nor would I change facts to better suit the story. Yet there are places where I have made assumptions or extrapolations about what likely occurred, based on information provided by those close to the event or on my own experience of backcountry skiing in the area.

The more I learned about the six individuals who died in this avalanche, the more I wished I had had the opportunity to know them. I hope that their families will take some solace from the thought that others may learn from their loss.

A NOTE TO American readers:

Canada uses the metric system of measurements, as does every other industrialized country in the world except for the United States. However, even American scientists working in the avalanche field employ metric units to measure what they find in their snowpits or beneath the snow's surface. It made sense for this book to use metric units, too, rather than Imperial units except for measurements in the U.S., such as mountain heights. For those who wish to do a rough conversion: there are about 2.5 centimeters to an inch, a kilometer is slightly farther than half a mile, a meter is just over three feet, and 0° Celsius equals 32° Fahrenheit, freezing level.

{Prologue}

*

January 2, 1998

MORE THAN 30 centimeters of fresh snow had fallen over the past twenty-four hours in this area of the Selkirk Mountains. Winds from the north had swept further snow over the ridges onto south-facing slopes. Now, on this crisp, sparkly morning, a vast expanse of untracked powder stretched from the rim of a huge alpine basin down to the broad flats more than a kilometer below.

Six tiny figures entered the basin from the west, dwarfed by the mountains. One at a time they skied down onto a natural bench that broke up the steeper sections of the basin.

The fresh snow rested atop a snowpack that had been accumulating since the first drifting flakes of winter. It was now well over a meter deep, an interconnected mass of tiny ice grains. But within this mass were also unconsolidated layers of sugary crystals. Given enough encouragement, the top section of the snowpack could shear loose at one of these weak layers. Especially on the steepest slopes around the rim of the bowl, it wouldn't take much of a jolt to initiate a slide. But for the moment, the snow held together, a soft white blanket beneath a cold blue sky.

The first indication of trouble may have been a "whumph" as the snowpack beneath the travelers' skis settled a few cenimeters. That would be the sound of the upper slab collapsing into loose crystals below, shooting air out of the snowpack. The skiers may have actually seen the snow drop beneath their feet. From where they were standing, they may also have felt shock waves shoot across the slope, as the shear at the weak layer propagated through the snowpack. Fast as lightning, those shock waves sped up to the steep slopes far above. That's where the snowpack finally lost its grip.

One moment the blanket of snow was still intact. Then, as if slashed by a giant knife, a crack split open across the upper slope, ripping around the rim of the bowl. The snow below the fracture line started to release, a slab that broke into blocks that crumbled and shattered, scooping up more snow as the slide accelerated. In moments, the avalanche had become a chaotic torrent. Thousands of tonnes of snow hurtled down the basin. The avalanche overran a first bench, then a second, smoking down the slope at the speed of a freight train. Where rock outcrops funneled the bowl into a chute, cascading snow from all sides of the basin converged, blasting through cliffs, ripping off branches, uprooting stumps and shooting debris missiles into the air and out to the side. Finally, the snow spilled out on the flat run-out zone, successive waves piling up from behind to form an enormous heap. When the avalanche stopped, its energy spent, the heat generated by billions of snow crystals crashing together dissipated. Individual crystals froze together, and the snow set up like concrete.

It was all over in thirty seconds or so. Nobody could out-run something like that.

{1}

THUMBS UP

Saturday, December 27, 1997

LISE NICOLA threw her duffel bag and daypack into the back of her dark blue Mazda pickup, where they joined her skis, poles, boots and an assortment of cardboard boxes. She briefly contemplated the pile—did she have everything? All that was on her list, anyhow. She slammed the tailgate shut.

Nicola let the old truck warm up while she scraped frost off the windshield. A small woman, she had to stand on her toes to reach across the hood. Once the windshield was clear, she climbed into her truck, popped a Tom Petty tape into the tape deck and rolled down the driveway, tires crunching on packed-down snow. She set off along the secondary roads leading to Highway 3A, following the Kootenay River upstream towards Nelson, 10 kilometers away.

The streets of Nelson were quiet at 8:00 AM on the day after Boxing Day, with most residents indulging in post-Christmas lethargy. The downhill skiers would soon be heading towards the Whitewater ski hill a half-hour's drive out of town, but since there hadn't been any fresh snow for a week, there wasn't going to be the usual rush for first tracks. Snow conditions weren't anything to rave about in the backcountry, either, unfortunately. Unlike Nicola, most of the Nelsonites who normally sought out untracked slopes there might decide to stay home and do chores today.

Nelson, located in the mountainous West Kootenay region of southeastern British Columbia, was built on a hillside above an arm of Kootenay Lake, where the lake narrows to form the outflowing river. The streets tilt towards the water and turn into luge runs after a fresh snowfall. Some uphill residents strap crampons onto their boots for the walk to their downtown offices. Nelson always looks like a storybook illustration in winter, with its heritage buildings, old-fashioned lamp posts and ye olde street signs. It is the kind of setting location scouts love for movie shoots—Steve Martin sang its praises after he and Darryl Hannah completed the film *Roxanne* there in 1987. Afterwards, tourists would arrive in town to take the "Roxanne" walking tour.

Once based on mining and logging revenues, Nelson's economy is now a diversified mix of regional government offices, tourism, services and cultural activity. There's a big arts contingent—quiz virtually anyone waiting on tables and you'll find a part-time dancer, artisan, musician or writer working to pay the bills. Art schools blossom despite government cutbacks, the walls of local stores and restaurants display paintings and photographs, and the 1920s art-deco theater has been restored to its red plush and gilt glory.

To the chagrin of its more conservative residents, the area is also renowned for its alternative lifestyle contingent. Downtown businesses include a thriving organic food cooperative and shops selling hemp and ethically produced wares. Posters promote a bewildering variety of yoga classes and "rebalancing" sessions that have nothing to do with automotive tires. There's a lucrative underground cannabis industry.

But especially, Nelson is known for its mountain and lakeshore setting. Help-wanted ads cite the region's recreational opportunities as a lure to attract professionals to the city. The downtown boasts a disproportionate number of outdoor equipment retail stores, exceeded only by the number of coffee hangouts. Winter attractions include a little ski hill that gets raves in ski magazines, as well as easy access to the backcountry. With all this to recommend it, Nelson, population nine thousand, regularly makes it onto the lists of best North American small towns to live in or visit.

Nelson had been Lise Nicola's base for the past six years. She had discovered that the place perfectly suited her lifestyle, with mountains at her doorstep and plenty of like-minded outdoorsy folks.

Nicola cruised along tree-lined streets, then stopped for a red light at one of the six traffic signals in town. On one corner of the intersection was the Heritage Inn, touted as "The Largest and Finest Hostelry in the Interior of the Province" when it opened for business in 1898. City Hall across the street, built in 1902, looked like a miniature Disney castle in pink brick with a round turret and flag on top. On the opposite corner was the ivy-covered stone courthouse, a Late Victorian edifice with a massive arch over the entrance. The "Queen City of the Kootenays," incorporated over one hundred years earlier, still had pretensions.

Continuing downhill towards the lake, Nicola peered through her foggy windshield at the snowy mountain peaks on the far side. In two hours she'd be up there, at the Silver Spray cabin in Kokanee Glacier Provincial Park. She couldn't tell from the lake what the visibility would be like up on the mountain, and she knew that Keith Westfall, the helicopter pilot, wouldn't even take off from Nelson if he didn't think he had a good chance of getting in. But it looked clear enough to fly today, she thought, and once they were safely installed in the cabin for the week, who cared what the weather did. Let it snow!

It was part of Nicola's job as cabin custodian to make sure that the skiers flying up to Silver Spray with her that morning were at the helicopter base in time for the mandatory pre-flight safety briefing. There would be six, apart from her: two women and four men. Nicola already knew a couple of the locals, and she'd talked to several of the others on the phone.

Pulling into the parking area beside the helicopter base, Nicola nosed her front bumper up to the chain-link fence, shut off the engine and hopped out. She immediately started the job of carrying her skis and the rest of her baggage towards the Jet Ranger, which waited like a giant dragonfly on the tarmac.

Keith Westfall was busy with his pre-flight walkaround, visually inspecting the outside of the machine, opening and shutting engine doors, checking oil levels, eyeing the main rotor mast and the blades. He wore snow boots, a warm jacket and nylon wind pants over his jeans. Inside the helicopter it would be warm enough, but a pilot had to be prepared in case of unexpected landings in the mountains. Westfall greeted Nicola and asked her how many passengers would be flying up. He needed to calculate fuel quantities, not wanting to carry any more than was required.

By 8:30 all of the skiers had arrived at the heliport, although some were still scurrying about sealing cardboard food boxes shut with duct tape and jamming last-minute items into backpacks and athletic bags. Excitement and anticipation filled the air. This group had won the lottery—literally. Rob Driscoll, a local physician with a passion for mountains, had entered the draw for a week at one of the two ski cabins in Kokanee Glacier Park, and his name had been pulled from a pile of over a hundred applicants. Driscoll had moved to Nelson just a year earlier with Carrie Fitzsimons, a pediatrician; the town was a perfect fit for his long ponytail and his enthusiasm for outdoor adventures. Driscoll and Fitzsimons had met in Iqaluit, Baffin Island, capital of Canada's northern territory now known as Nunavut, while they were both doing locums there. Nelson seemed an ideal place to balance work and play, far from the big-city grind, so they'd chosen to settle there. Although Fitzsimons didn't share Driscoll's love of mountain climbing, and only scrambled with him "under duress," she loved camping and the outdoors, and she was an avid downhill skier. Less than a month before, they had married on a beach in Hawaii, and now they would be spending New Year's at a cabin high in the snowy alpine.

Driscoll had asked a local couple he knew to join them on the trip. Patrick Von Blumen, who worked for a Nelson distributor of outdoor products, had grown up on the North Shore of Vancouver, British Columbia, at the base of the mountains overlooking the city, but he'd moved to Nelson to escape the city scene. Von Blumen was a man who radiated energy, standing out from any crowd with his strong presence, chiseled Germanic features, blond hair and blue eyes.

13

His girlfriend, Mary Cowan, was the only one of the group to have grown up in Nelson; her family owned an office supply business there. Cowan was a lively, free-spirited redhead who had worked as a ski patroller at the hill.

Von Blumen, in turn, invited a couple of good friends from his boyhood years in North Vancouver to come along. One was Geoffrey Leidal, known to many as "Lumpy," a gregarious, high-energy soul who lived in the Whistler area of British Columbia, two hours north of Vancouver. Whistler, one of North America's primo downhill skiing and recreation destinations, is packed with ritzy hotels and condos for the wealthy, but it has a resident population of hard-core outdoor aficionados who wait on tables, work in construction and hit the slopes at every opportunity. Leidal worked as a carpenter, building graceful timber log houses with lots of curved lines. He'd spent Christmas in Whistler with his parents, and even on Christmas Day he was still trying to decide whether he was actually going to go on the ski trip to Silver Spray. But Von Blumen had called and, in his forthright way, urged Leidal to live up to his commitments. Leidal set off on Boxing Day, heading first for North Vancouver and then driving up from there with another of Von Blumen's friends, Scott Bradley.

The car must have vibrated with their combined energy. Bradley was another guy who operated at full-throttle, with a great sense of humor and a love of fun. He was an avid mountain biker as well as a keen kayaker. Backcountry skiing was a relatively new pursuit for him, but he was open to almost any experience, particularly if it got him out of the office. Bradley enjoyed meeting people and seemed to genuinely care what they had to say. And he loved to cut up. Already, as the ski group waited on the tarmac for their safety briefing, he and

Lumpy were providing the entertainment. Watching Bradley's boyish antics, one might not have guessed that he was also a solid businessman, owner of an air-conditioning and heating installation company with a dozen employees, many of them much older than he was.

Both Bradley and Mary Cowan had encouraged a mutual acquaintance, Shannon Hames, to join them on the trip. Hames had thought seriously about it, but since she was inexperienced in the backcountry, she would be relying on the guidance of others. She didn't really know most of the people in this group of skiers, so in the end she opted out.

Two others who had planned to be on the trip also decided at the last minute to drop out. Linda Kalbun, an occupational therapist, and Anna Reid, a Nelson physician who worked with Fitzsimons and Driscoll at the Kootenay Lake Regional Hospital, had become apprehensive about snow and weather conditions at the Silver Spray cabin. Reid had phoned around to get the opinion of some seasoned local skiers, and what she heard wasn't encouraging. The forecast called for a big dump of snow and winds from the north, which would load the south-facing lee slopes. The area had a bit of a reputation for avalanches in conditions like that. Kalbun figured they would spend a lot of time holed up in the cabin. The issue was decided when Reid came down with the flu just before they were set to leave. Kalbun and Reid bailed.

That left a group of six: the two couples from Nelson and the two men from the coast. The skiers gathered around the chopper as Keith Westfall began his safety briefing. It's easy for inexperienced passengers stoked by adrenalin to get flustered or overexcited when close to a helicopter, with its deafening noise and gale-force rotor wash. But nobody should play loose around a blade rotating at 394 revolutions per minute. "Don't be in a hurry just because the helicopter is running," Westfall told them. "By hurrying you may save fifteen seconds, but something is more likely to go wrong."

Among his non-negotiable rules: Never walk behind the helicopter, where the tail rotor, spinning so fast it's invisible, could slice through a body. Don't assume that the swirling overhead rotor blades are well above head height; in a wind they can tilt to one side. Never raise items above the head; they might get pushed into that overhead rotor. One previous ski group had accidentally tossed a portable camp chair into the revolving blades—an expensive mistake at $45,000 a blade. Instead, skis and long objects should be dragged along the snow.

Westfall explained how to latch the doors without slamming them and how to do up the four-point lap belts and additional shoulder belts once inside. He showed the passengers where the emergency locator transmitter, the first aid kit and the survival kit were stored.

When they loaded, Westfall's boss would be on hand to pack the gear into the baggage compartment on the left side of the helicopter, but one of Driscoll's group would be in charge of putting the skis into the long metal basket on the other side, Westfall told them. Lise Nicola and the outgoing hut custodian at Silver Spray would help with the unloading. "When you disembark from the helicopter, crouch down in the snow beside the machine where I can see you," continued Westfall. Once he got a thumbs-up signal from the hut keepers and started to lift off, the skiers should be prepared to hold down any lightweight objects that might go for a sail in the rotor wash.

Only Nicola would fly with the pilot on the first gear load to the Silver Spray cabin. The rest of the group would drive

50 kilometers north, along the winding lakeshore highway, to a helicopter staging area much closer to their mountain destination. After depositing Nicola, Westfall would fly back down to that staging area to ferry the two loads of passengers.

The safety talk completed, Westfall checked by radio with the custodian at the Silver Spray cabin to get an update on the weather and visibility there. On occasion groups had been forced to wait three or four days before they could fly in, but today conditions were good. Westfall and Nicola packed a full load into the chopper, while the other skiers carted the remaining baggage to their cars to take with them up the lake. They were overweight with their freight, thanks to the generous allotment of wine and food they'd brought, and were going to have to pay for an extra helicopter flight.

Nicola and Westfall were soon flying high above Kootenay Lake, heading north towards the mountains of the park. The long lake is walled by mountains—the Purcell Range on the east, the Selkirk Range on the west. The chopper flew over the Selkirks, rising steadily over thick forests that segued into alpine slopes. Kokanee Glacier Park encompasses more than 32,000 hectares of spectacular, largely undeveloped mountain wilderness. It is a sea of alpine peaks and ridges, glaciers, frozen lakes and wildlife, from pikas to bears, now ensconced in their winter dens. Most of the park is above 1800 meters in elevation; half is above 2100. Kokanee Peak, the mountain smack dab in the center, is 2774 meters high.

Nicola had spent the past two summers as a park ranger, keeping watch over visiting hikers and resident grizzlies, tracking use demographics, and maintaining trails, wilderness campsites and cabins. The day she learned she had been hired for that job was one of the happiest of her life. Her first visit to the Silver Spray area, in the northeast corner of the park, had been three years earlier, when she hiked up the steep, 1000-meter summer trail with her friend Angelina Eisele to join a work party raising the frame for a new cabin there. She was looking forward to spending the upcoming week at that beautiful cabin, now completed, and to skiing the nearby slopes.

The Selkirk Mountains are known for unlimited mountain terrain and, thanks to the moist winter climate, gobs of snow. Other places in North America might market themselves more aggressively (Utah licencse plates claim the state has the "Greatest Snow on Earth"), but the skiing in the Selkirks is as good as it gets. Every weekend, clusters of four-wheel-drive trucks and SUVs are parked at the top of plowed logging roads or along the side of the highways that crest the mountain passes—wherever there is access to high-elevation backcountry slopes. Some skiers use snowmobiles to roar up old mining tracks or logging roads. But for the ultimate Selkirk experience, skiers tuck themselves away in cabins high in the mountains, such as the two cabins in Kokanee Glacier Park. You can ski your heart out day after day and never see another soul. It's ski heaven.

Rob Driscoll's group had booked the Silver Spray cabin. Another party of skiers (from Utah, unaccountably) had booked the cabin called the Slocan Chief. The huts were in different sections of the park, separated by about seven kilometers of jagged ridges, glaciated peaks and steep valleys. For one week, each group of skiers would be isolated in its remote mountain hideaway, far removed from the stress of jobs and the demands of cellphones, alarm clocks and traffic snarls. Instead, they would bask in silence and solitude. Life would be brought back to the basics—eating, sleeping, spending time with friends and skiing.

Lotteries were used at both cabins to fill the twenty-four one-week time slots between December and May. In all, several hundred visitors skied from Silver Spray and the Slocan Chief during a typical winter. The lucky skiers are flown in by chopper, since the only other means of access was a lengthy uphill slog on skis, following unplowed summer-access roads and trails. Once there, the skiers were self-reliant, doing their own cooking and making their own judgments about which slopes to ski. A paid custodian in each cabin cut wood, shoveled paths, recorded weather observations and took care of radio communications. The custodians promoted basic safety practices, but there were no guides; groups had to be experienced enough to fend for themselves in the winter mountains.

Lise Nicola and Keith Westfall had been in the air for almost twenty minutes, floating across the alpine landscape. Westfall checked by radio to get updates on weather and visibility conditions at the cabin. Then, suddenly the ground beneath the helicopter dropped and they were flying over a deep, forested trench, with Woodbury Creek visible far below. Across the drop, a rock outcrop jutted out from the mountain slope, high above the valley. Perched on top was the small, square helipad, marked with flagged stakes. Several figures in parkas and toques, who had been watching the machine descend, turned their backs to shield themselves from the blast of helicopter wash. Edging in slowly, Westfall settled the machine down on the vertiginous platform. A few dozen meters away, protected by the outcrop and appearing tiny in the surrounding landscape, was the two-story Silver Spray cabin.

With the rotor slicing the air overhead, Nicola climbed out and started unloading gear from her side of the helicopter,

19

handing the boxes to those who had come forward to help. One member of the waiting group approached the other side of the machine, in a crouch, to unload the skis from the long metal basket. He motioned four people forward to take their seats in the helicopter, checking their seatbelts before latching the doors shut. The Jet Ranger could take three passengers in the back and one up front with the pilot. That done, the man gave Westfall the thumbs-up signal, then sprawled across the unloaded gear to keep it grounded as the machine lifted off in a swirl of powder, diving down into the Woodbury Creek valley to exchange its passengers for the first four members of Rob Driscoll's group waiting below. As the throbbing subsided, Lise Nicola stood up with her trademark smile to greet her good friend Sean McTague.

McTague had helped Nicola learn the ropes when she started working as a ranger in the park. He had dark hair and smiling Irish eyes, a man originally from Ontario who had been lured west by the mountains. McTague had admired his new recruit's quick mind and the enthusiasm, determination and thoroughness with which she'd tackled her tasks. During her first days on the job, he had put her to work building timber-frame benches for the cabins, something she had never done before. After he explained the process and was laying out the pieces to be cut, she pointed out that he was doing it wrong, at least according to what he'd just told her. She was a fast study, McTague had ruefully concluded. Nicola was also fun to work with; she was always coming back from some outdoor adventure or other on her days off, so she had lots to talk about.

McTague had been staying at the cabin for several days over Christmas to prepare Silver Spray for the winter season.

He would be flying out today on the last flight. But as one of the rotating cabin custodians, he'd be back again in a week.

He and Nicola caught up on news as they hauled gear from the helicopter landing area down the shoveled path to the cabin. He updated her on the unstable snow conditions his group had been experiencing during the past few days. She told him how school was going. McTague had encouraged her to finish her teaching degree, and that fall she had been doing a practicum in a split grade five and six class in Nelson. The students had just studied a novel set in the Kootenay area, and Nicola had regaled them with her own depictions of some caves and other locations mentioned in the book. She had earned a degree in environmental studies six years before, but she had tried on an assortment of short-term and seasonal jobs before settling on this long-term path. Being introduced to the backcountry was the greatest gift she had received as a youth, and she wanted to pass on her passion and enthusiasm for the outdoors to other kids. She had started filling cardboard boxes with great ideas for projects she could do with her future students.

While McTague and Nicola were exchanging stories, Rob Driscoll's group was waiting below for the chopper. The helicopter pad was on the grounds of the Woodbury Resort, a rustic fishing lodge located just where Woodbury Creek, originating deep within Kokanee Glacier Park, spills into the west side of Kootenay Lake. The cluster of red-and-white painted buildings sits among tall fir and cedar trees—a lodge, some cabins, a campsite (deserted at this time of year), a marina and a restaurant-pub known for great halibut and fries. As a whirlybird flies, it was a short hop, four minutes and 1850 meters vertical, from the lakeshore to the Silver Spray cabin.

On the other side of the lake, patchy cloud clung to the steep, forested slopes.

While waiting, the skiers were able to find out a bit more about each other. Rob Driscoll hadn't previously met Lumpy Leidal, although he had heard of him. In North Vancouver and Whistler circles, Leidal had a reputation as a wild and adventurous spirit who cranked up adrenalin and pushed the edge, whether on a snowboard, on skis, on a mountain bike or in a kayak. After he almost drowned on one kayak outing, he described to his mother exactly what kind of wake he wanted in the event of his early demise. She asked him not to tell her about future adventures until he was safely home again.

Leidal would regularly rise at 5:00 AM and go for a killer bike ride with his dog to burn off energy before showing up at his construction job, where he would work at breakneck speed. He had begun to mellow and mature of late, compared to his younger self, but he still promised to be an entertaining and colorful addition to the group.

As Leidal learned, Driscoll also had a few adventures under his belt. Raised in West Vancouver, he was already scrambling up impressive peaks as a teenager, and he became one of the youngest to summit 4019-meter-high Mount Waddington, the highest mountain in the British Columbia Coast Range. Driscoll had since climbed all over the world, from Yosemite's walls to Africa's Mount Kenya. He and a fellow climber achieved the first ascent by North Americans of Jannu, a remote and difficult 7710-meter Himalayan peak in Nepal.

Climbing was his passion, but Driscoll was also a kayaker, a paraglider, a mountain biker and a telemark skier. He just wanted to be out there, and he felt at peace in the mountains. A good conversationalist with an unassuming, upbeat manner and a wicked sense of humor, he was exactly the kind of guy you might choose to be stuck with in a snowbound cabin. His medical expertise was a plus.

Whoppa, whoppa, whoppa. The helicopter appeared overhead, the noise making verbal communication next to impossible. Driscoll and the others hastily pulled their hoods forward and hunkered down to shield themselves and their belongings from the chopper blizzard. They patted their pockets to make sure that their mitts and toques were handy. It would be 10 degrees colder on the mountain.

The skids of the helicopter settled down onto the flats beside the lake, and four of Driscoll's group traded places with the skiers coming off the mountain. Westfall's employer had turned up to collect the fees for the flight, and now he helped with loading and unloading. The pilot waited to see his boss signal "thumbs-up" before lifting the machine from the pad, tilting forward and taking off across the lake. The helicopter swept in a large half-circle to gain elevation before flying back overhead and disappearing up the thickly timbered drainage of Woodbury Creek. Those left behind at the lakeshore exhaled.

In a few minutes, the helicopter alighted again on the helipad beside the Silver Spray cabin. The passengers piled out and crouched while McTague and Nicola pulled out baggage. Then Westfall was off again, returning fifteen minutes later with the remaining members of the party.

Sean McTague flew out on the last flight after wishing the skiers a good week; he was heading home to Nelson. The helicopter disappeared down the valley. After all the planning and preparation, the last-minute problems to deal with, the long drive for some of them up from the coast . . . the group was finally in the mountains. Big smiles and high-fives all round.

The Silver Spray area once echoed with the shouts of miners working on the boulder-strewn hillside above, where dark shafts, a few weathered timbers and a rusty wheelbarrow still lay under the snow. Mining fever had hit the West Kootenays in the late 1800s, and many of the backcountry ski cabins in the area were originally mining shacks. Miners hauling ore and supplies had forged trails into the mountains. They were sometimes following paths created by the Sinixt and Ktunaxa peoples, who for thousands of years paddled the rivers and lakes of the region and wintered in subterranean pit houses along its waterways. The miners clambered over the steep mountain slopes looking for promising outcrops containing lead, silver and zinc. In some areas the winter snows were so deep that packhorses had to be fitted with snowshoes. Avalanches often swept away both mines and men. The railways that were soon built, clinging to the mountainsides, were also frequently buried by snow slides.

The Silver Spray cabin, a volunteer effort spearheaded by the Friends of West Kootenay Parks, was a timber-frame structure with a steep roofline and large south-facing windows. It replaced the smoky bunkhouse, circa 1920s, that had previously occupied the site. A photo of the original shack was mounted at the cabin's entrance.

Pat Von Blumen and Lise Nicola had skied at Silver Spray before, but the others were seeing the terrain for the first time. Sunrise Mountain rose to the northeast of the cabin, black granite thrusting vertically above the headwall of Clover Basin. Mount McQuarrie, higher at 2688 meters, stood about a kilometer to the northwest. A col, the low point in the saddle between those two peaks, served as the gateway to what the group knew from their topographic maps were more ski slopes on the permanently glaciated north side.

But the mind-expanding view was to the south. A vast panorama of mountains stretched into the blue beyond, crowding the horizon. At the skiers' feet, the slope dropped more than a thousand meters into the forested valley of Woodbury Creek. Across that valley they could identify Pontiac Peak and other prominent features of the park. The dark waters of Kootenay Lake were visible in the distance, with the peaks of the Purcell Mountains beyond.

Tectonic plate collisions starting some 180 million years earlier had laid the foundation for this dramatic setting. The subsequent advance and retreat of ice sheets over millions of years, followed by wind, water and ice erosion, had further chiseled the terrain. Here, unlike on the eastern side of the continent, the landscape still reflected the immensity of the geologic forces that had sculpted it. A giant blanket of white covered everything, broken only by patches of dark rock cliff and vertical pinnacles that had shrugged off the snow.

The landscape was spectacular, no doubt about it. But there would be plenty of time for gawking later. For now, the group got to work hauling the remaining boxes and packs from the helipad down to the cabin. They knocked the snow off their boots before setting their loads down in the kitchen area. The main floor was one large room, with pine benches and a table at one end, green arborite counters and a propane cooking stove at the other. A drying rack hung over wood- and propane-fired heaters sitting in the center. A ladder led to the airy loft, where guests laid down their sleeping bags on foam mattresses.

This was their temporary home, a small shelter in a wonderfully silent landscape of rock and snow. High above the madding crowd, they were in another world, another state of being. They began to settle in.

{2}

FIRST FLAKES

*

A T THE START OF every winter, British Columbia's West Kootenays hum with snow fever. "Did you see the dusting of white on the peaks?" "Think this will be an early ski year?" "Buying any new equipment this season?"

The weather systems that bring snow to the region generally blow in from the Pacific. Propelled by a rapidly flowing river of air known as the mid-latitude jet stream, maritime storms slam into the British Columbia coast from the southwest and embark on a roller coaster ride over the province's mountain ranges. As a general rule, the coastal storms drop moisture on the westerly slopes, leaving the lee slopes in rain shadow.

The first barrier faced by the incoming weather systems are the Coast Mountains, which rise abruptly from inlets along the Pacific Ocean to form a 300-kilometer-wide wall from the United States border to the Alaskan Panhandle. The frontal assault leaves the coast with North America's heaviest rainfalls. At higher elevations, this precipitation falls as snow—and lots of it.

The weather systems pick up more moisture as they sweep east over the large lakes and rivers of B.C.'s rolling interior plateau. Their next barrier is the Columbia Mountains, a broad belt of peaks that stretches north to south for 600 kilometers through southeastern British Columbia, with the Selkirk Range forming its backbone. There, the weather systems drench the windward slopes with rain or snow. A temperate rainforest cloaks lower-elevation slopes of the Selkirks with tall cedars, hemlocks and stalks of devil's club.

Inland of the Columbia Mountains lies the Rocky Mountain Trench, a U-shaped trough that forms the largest valley in North America. On the far side of the trench are the Rockies themselves, straddling the southern border between British Columbia and Alberta and stretching south into the United States. By the time storm systems pile into these mountains, they've just about wrung themselves out. That leaves the Rockies with long droughts between storms and a shallower winter snowpack.

By November, storms are usually hammering the Selkirk Mountain slopes. Keeners who don't mind leaving scrapings from their ski bases on the occasional rock are already carving turns in the snow on the higher slopes in late November and early December.

But the winter of 1997–98 was an odd one. It was an El Niño year, when disturbances in the tropical Pacific were blamed for disastrous weather events throughout the globe—floods in California, twisters in central Florida, ice storms in eastern Canada and the United States, fires in southeast Asia and Mexico, and plummeting fish stocks off the coast of Peru.

In the Selkirks, it meant an abnormally warm start to the winter, with almost zilch in the way of snowfall. The Pacific weather systems were being deflected up the coast to the north, leaving the interior of southern British Columbia high and dry. The mean temperature in early winter was the warmest since 1987. The weather office at Castlegar airport, 40 kilometers from Nelson, reported just a couple of dustings of snow in November, compared to 127 centimeters at that time the year before. There was more snow at higher elevations, but overall the precipitation was only 33 per cent of normal.

Early December was similarly dry: the area received less than half the normal amount of precipitation. Local powder hounds were going squirrely. Ski guides became uneasy, knowing that shallow snowpacks often become avalanche prone. When the snow cover is thin, and temperatures drop, the stage is set for an interesting transformation to take place beneath the snow.

Without an insulating blanket of cloud, the clear skies of early December promoted rapid nighttime cooling. The ground temperature at the bottom of the snowpack remained at about 0°C, because snow is such a good insulator, but the air temperature at the surface plunged to well below freezing each night.

Because the snowpack was so shallow, the difference in temperature between the ground and the surface formed a steep gradient. The air at ground level held more water vapor than the colder air higher up. Gases tend to move from areas of high concentration to areas of low concentration, so this moist air percolated up through the snowpack into the atmosphere. As it cooled, it deposited ice on the bottom of individual snow grains, eventually building them up into large angular crystals with faceted faces. Instead of a tightly interlocked base of co-hesive snow, the bottom of the snowpack became a mass of loose crystals called depth hoar. It was as if the snowpack had rotted from underneath.

Faceted crystals don't bond well. They are like sugar—in-dividual grains that flow through the fingers—and won't pack into a decent snowball. These faceted crystals form unconsol-idated, weak layers in the snow where the snowpack can come unglued.

One of the people monitoring the West Kootenay snow-pack developments that winter was Nelson's Dave Smith. As avalanche control expert for the provincial government's highways department, Smith monitors the snow-laden slopes that threaten the region's major roads. When the slopes are potentially hazardous, he becomes a helicopter-borne bom-bardier, dropping explosives to trigger controlled slides. It is a job small boys can only dream about.

Smith is not a suit-and-tie kind of guy. He has the look of someone who spends a lot of time outdoors, with a weathered face, very blue eyes and short, graying hair that appears to be permanently windblown. In the 1970s he earned his living as a mountain guide, but after he and his wife, Molly, had their first child in 1976, they opened a ski shop so that Smith could be home nights. Smith never really liked it, though, and he was still guiding in the Rockies in the summer. When an ava-lanche control position with the provincial highways depart-ment came up, it seemed to offer his family a measure of security (by then, he and Molly had three kids), yet dovetailed nicely with summer guiding. During the twenty-two years he's been doing the job, he's seen a lot of snow fly and run through many avalanche cycles.

A large part of avalanche prediction involves identifying layers of faceted crystals in the snowpack and estimating how much additional load or stress they can handle before they shear. Any time Smith identifies suspect layers in his snow-pits, he digs and probes at other sites to see how prevalent these layers are throughout the region. As the winter progresses, he makes educated guesses about when those layers might become overloaded. Sometimes weak layers are bridged by icy crusts that distribute the load over a wider area, so the snowpack can withstand additional weight.

Smith also tries to get a handle on how far an avalanche is likely to propagate under current snow conditions. Will it just release beneath the trigger point? Or is the upper snowpack developing into a cohesive slab, allowing tension to build up over a widespread area? In the latter case, a collapse or fracture at the weak layer in one spot could send shock waves shooting tremendous distances, causing a very broad avalanche or a succession of avalanches across the slope.

It is somewhat unusual for Smith to see depth hoar in the Selkirks, which tend to have a deep, stable snowpack, regularly receiving snow accumulations of three meters or more. Depth hoar is common in the Rockies, which are notorious for shallow snowpacks and cold temperatures. But on the coast, where the mountains usually receive buckets of snow, depth hoar is virtually unknown. Even if the area is hit by an arctic air mass, causing air temperatures to plummet, the deeper snowpack ensures that the temperature gradient between ground and surface will be gentle, and therefore not conducive to facet formation. In a relatively warm and deep snowpack, water vapor tends to round the snowflakes instead, gluing them together. What you gain in stability you lose in snow quality—this is not a recipe for light, fluffy powder. Generally, though, the snowpack sets up better in the coastal mountains, becoming consolidated and stable. It's a misconception that the avalanche risk is higher where snow is deeper and heavier. The opposite is often the case: drier years can be deadly ones.

Although depth hoar isn't common in the Selkirks, however, it can form anywhere early in the season when the snowpack is still shallow. On December 8, 1997, the public avalanche bulletin issued by the Canadian Avalanche Centre (CAC) noted a layer of facets forming at the base of the shallow snowpack in numerous areas in the south Columbia Mountains, including the Selkirks. The bulletin also called attention to another potentially nasty feature backcountry travelers should watch for—surface hoar.

Surface hoar is a fancy name for frost. The large, feathery crystals grow on the surface of the snow on clear nights when there is little or no wind to blow them away. They are magical, dazzling and sparkling like diamonds when the sun reflects off them. But when blanketed by subsequent snowfalls, a surface hoar layer becomes treacherous, since it bonds poorly with the snow above and below. An analysis of fifty-five fatal avalanches in Canada showed that a third of them slid on a layer of surface hoar.

Buried facets and hoar layers can become either more or less of a threat as winter progresses. From the time it forms in early winter to the time it melts in late spring, the snowpack is constantly freezing, thawing, settling and morphing. Differences in temperature and air pressure keep water molecules on the move, changing the shape of the crystals and making the snow weaker or stronger. When individual snow grains bond or glob together (a process known as sintering), they form little links called necks. Like Tinkertoy connections, these links give the snow strength and stability.

But the faceted layers that form early in the winter can also linger within the snowpack, even for the whole season, waiting to reveal themselves under the right set of circumstances. Sometimes, fortunately, those circumstances don't occur. But each subsequent snowfall further stresses the weak bonds in those layers—ensuring that an avalanche, if it happens, will be even bigger and more destructive.

Dave Smith couldn't say how this winter in the Selkirks would unfold, but the foundation was being laid down now: depth hoar, surface hoar and facets. Nobody likes to see a snowpack like that at the beginning of the season.

THE FIRST SIGNIFICANT winter storms finally blew across the south Columbia Mountains in mid-December. There would be a white Christmas after all. The avalanche center bulletin for December 18 reported storm snow accumulations of up to half a meter. Skiers were jubilant, although this topload of warmer snow was definitely putting stress on the weaker layers of faceted crystals below. The snow still clung to the slopes, but it might not take much to trigger a release.

"So we have a situation," the bulletin read, "where there are a variety of Rockies-like characteristics that are waiting for adequate load to avalanche naturally or with the additional weight of a snow traveler." In some areas, buried surface hoar and facets lay just above or just below icy crust layers that would make slick sliding surfaces for an avalanche. "A 10 to 20 centimeter layer of facets is reported on the ground for many areas," the bulletin noted. That was the depth hoar, still lurking at the base of the snowpack. There was also some cracking and whumphing. ("Whumpf" is a term that the Canadian Avalanche Association has officially adopted to describe the sound of a fracture propagating along a buried weak layer. The noise—however you spell it—occurs when, deep in the snowpack, an unconsolidated layer containing large air pockets collapses, and the denser snow above settles into that air space.) Given the conditions, the avalanche hazard was classified as "Considerable," midway between Moderate and High, meaning that human-triggered avalanches were probable and skiers should take caution on steeper terrain.

The CAC bulletin's "Weekly Award for Stunning Event" went to a kilometer-and-a-half-long fracture line that had shot across slopes in Kootenay Pass, about 50 kilometers south of Nelson. The event indicated that the upper snowpack was becoming cohesive, and hence that avalanches could propagate. Snowpack conditions would vary from one location to the next. But anyone skiing in the Selkirks over the holiday would need to pay close attention to the hazards lying underfoot.

{3}

AVALANCHE EYEBALLS

*

NELSON SKI GUIDE Marc Deschenes was definitely planning to get some turns in over Christmas. On the morning of December 20, he and several friends flew by helicopter into Kokanee Glacier Park. Their destination was the other cabin in the park, the Slocan Chief, nestled in a subalpine forest near the toe of Kokanee Glacier. The hundred-year-old mining shack looked like a children's book illustration of a woodsman's cottage in the forest, with weathered logs and a mushroom cap of snow. The drafty building exuded character rather than comfort, providing spartan accommodation with wooden tables and benches and a dingy upstairs sleeping loft.

Deschenes, originally from Montreal, Quebec, had come west in the early 1980s as a geological engineering student, and he had been blown away by his first glimpse of the Rockies. The mountains were a treat for a young geologist—all that exposed rock right there in your face. And for an outdoors person, the opportunities for exploration were irresistible. Deschenes returned to British Columbia after finishing his degree and found work as a geologist. Summers in the field were fine, but to escape the boredom of winter office work, friends suggested that he become a certified ski guide. He got work with a heli-ski company, jumping in with both feet. Heli-skiing is a big-time show, with high-powered clients paying hefty money for vertical, a lot of time spent in avalanche terrain, and many lives on the line. Besides technical knowledge and good judgment, a guide needs to exude competence and credibility so that the Fortune 500 executives in his charge will respect his instructions. It's stressful work. But Deschenes, with his straightforward, down-to-earth manner and easy smile, soon earned a reputation for being sound, reliable and level-headed. As an ex-hockey player, he was strong and tough. He liked being with people, sharing experiences and passing on his knowledge, and he turned out to be a good teacher.

The heli-ski season wouldn't start until January, so Deschenes had entered his name into the Kokanee Glacier lottery. He got lucky. What better place to spend Christmas than with friends in a cabin in the mountains, far from the crunch of last-minute shopping? It was just too bad that the snow conditions weren't better.

From the Slocan Chief, skiers can access a variety of terrain, some steep and some gentle, some high-elevation and open, some lower down in the trees. Immediately to the southeast of the cabin, a wide-open slope rises a thousand meters towards huge granite outcrops dubbed Giant's Kneecap, the Battleship and the Pyramids. In good visibility, skiers can continue even farther afield to ski on Kokanee Glacier. Or they can head off from the cabin in a westerly direction, dropping onto frozen lakes and climbing the far slopes to ski runs off Outlook Peak.

Deschenes was glad that the area included a lot of safe tree skiing and moderately sloped terrain, because the snowpack sure didn't feel stable on the steep stuff. Every morning as he prepared to head out onto the slopes, he mentally considered which runs his group might ski that day, and which lines to avoid. Usually there was somewhere to go that wasn't exposed to risk, even if it was lower-angled or forested. By choosing their terrain carefully, they could avoid getting into trouble but still be out skiing.

Avalanches happen at particular times and in particular places for particular reasons. That means they can usually be avoided. In many cases, clues about the avalanche hazard abound for those who know where to look. As one avalanche educator puts it, you wouldn't cross a four-lane highway without listening for traffic and looking both ways; nor should you travel across steep, snow-covered slopes without gathering information about snow stability or the probability of avalanches. You may still be able to cross safely, but it's a matter of timing, wise decisions and safety precautions. Avalanche veterans Doug Fesler and Jill Fredston of the Alaskan Mountain Safety Center have come up with a diagram called the avalanche triangle, where the three sides represent three interrelating factors to which skiers should pay close attention: the terrain, the snowpack stability and the weather.

36   Experienced backcountry travelers are always on avalanche alert, observing their surroundings and soaking up a steady stream of data. They've developed what Doug Fesler calls "avalanche eyeballs." Whenever Marc Deschenes snapped his boots into his bindings, shouldered his pack and headed off up the slopes with his friends, he put his own ava-

lanche eyeballs to work. He did it almost subconsciously, although it's a process he had instilled many times in students in his avalanche courses. As he explains it, "I will put someone in the lead and I'm right behind them, and I question them on their route selection and what's going on in their mind, and the decisions they are making, and why. How is the leader making those decisions? What does he see in the terrain? What does he know about the snowpack? How is the weather influencing his decisions? Open your eyes—open your soul, for that matter—and take notes. There's so much going on."

In the first few days at Slocan Chief, Deschenes noted how deeply his skis penetrated the snowpack, a gauge of the depth and density of the new snow. He knew that snow-laden trees were a sign the snowpack hadn't had time to settle after a recent snowfall. By occasionally pushing the basket of his ski pole deep into the snow as he walked, he could measure the depth of the unconsolidated snow and feel for crusts and layers underneath. He could also tell whether or not those crusts were prevalent across the terrain.

As he gained elevation, Deschenes checked to see whether wind was becoming more of a factor. He watched for signs of wind loading—cornices drooping from ridge tops, tree trunks plastered on one side with snow, windblown "waves" on the snow's surface, and deep pillows or drifts. Wind sweeps loose snow from windward slopes over the ridges onto lee slopes, and the snow forms stiff slabs as the grains pack together. The addition of windblown deposits increases the weight of the overlying snow several-fold. It is a huge contributor to avalanches, and it catches many novices by surprise. Some old-timers say if you are a good judge of wind loading and slope steepness, you can avoid 90 per cent of slides.

Big avalanches are unlikely to run on really steep slopes, because the snow sluffs off continually and never has a chance to accumulate. Very shallow slopes don't avalanche either, because gravity pulls the snow to ground. It's the slopes of between 30 and 45 degrees that have the most potential for avalanches, and 38 degrees is just about prime.

After years of practice, Deschenes was pretty adept at estimating slope angles. Out with his friends that week, he set their uphill track so that it hugged the gentler inclines and followed the ridges, which tend to be less steep than the slopes on either side. His route sought out islands of safety in the terrain, such as thick glades of trees that anchored the snowpack or windward slopes that were scoured of snow. He continually looked up as they traveled, because avalanches can start on steeper terrain and tumble onto skiers moving across the flats. The idea was to minimize their exposure to slopes that could slide, and thus keep the odds in their favor.

Avalanche "sweet spots"—places where the snowpack is under particular stress—weren't always easy to detect. Something as subtle as a change in ground cover underneath the snow or a slightly shallower snowpack can make the difference. Avalanche pros joke about inventing "sweet spot goggles" that would allow them to look at a slope and clearly pinpoint trigger spots. Even without those magic goggles, though, Deschenes knew what kind of terrain to avoid when the snowpack was untrustworthy. Lee slopes where windblown snow added extra loading, steep slopes around the tops of bowls or on the downside of convex rolls where there's greater gravitational pull, faceted snow around warmer rocks—these are the places where the snow is under extra stress, or is likely to be particularly weak, or both.

As his group skied through the snowy landscape, Deschenes ran through various "What if?" scenarios. If a skier was caught and swept down that particular slope, what would be the consequences? A short ride onto flat ground or a plunge into a dangerous terrain trap—a gully, perhaps, or over a cliff? What would that south-facing slope be like later in the afternoon if the sun shone on it all day? What if there was a big dump of wet snow overnight—would that compress the snowpack and reduce the instability of those buried, loosely packed layers, or add to the stress on them? In his mind's eye he did some modeling, moving the wind around, carrying snow into potential avalanche starting zones, seeing the increasing hazards.

As Deschenes and his friends traveled, they looked for safe opportunities to test the slopes. If they found a small, steep incline where the consquences of a slide would be negligible, perhaps on the downhill side of a minor bump in the terrain, they would try jumping on it to see if that made the snowpack shear. Or, if there was a small opening in the forested slope, they would do a ski cut; one member of the party would ski quickly across the top of the opening between two points of safety, putting extra weight on his skis to try to trigger a slide. His momentum would carry him off the slide into the zone of safety if the slope actually let loose.

The group agreed the snow didn't feel trustworthy on the steeper terrain. Their weight often caused the snowpack surface to crack, a sign that it was forming a soft slab. They were also getting a lot of whumphing. The ominous sound made Deschenes's stomach do a little back flip. Sometimes he could actually feel the snowpack drop a few centimeters as the weak layer underlying the denser slab collapsed. On leveler ground, nothing would come of the snowpack shearing at this buried weak layer. But the shear could propagate and remotely trigger an avalanche on a steep slope above or some distance away.

To get a clearer picture of what was happening on slopes where they wanted to ski, Deschenes and his friends also dug snowpits, exposing a smooth cross-section of the snowpack. They isolated the various layers by rubbing the backs of their gloves over the wall of snow—the softer layers brushed away, whereas the harder ones resisted. By poking at the distinct layers, they could also gauge their hardness. An ideal snowpack becomes consistently denser and more consolidated with depth. That wasn't what they found. Beneath the topload of storm snow, the skiers noted faceted interfaces, where the snowpack could shear, and frozen crusts that would make smooth surfaces for a slide.

The group did further tests to gather information about the structure of the snowpack, the strength of the layers when placed under load, and the properties of the overriding slab. Most tests put stress on an isolated column of snow about the width of a shovel blade, cut out from the surrounding snowpack. The idea is to see what's needed to make the column shear at one of the weak interfaces. An upright shovel inserted at the back of the snow column, the blade flat against it, is used to gently pull the column horizontally out from the slope to see if it will shear. Compression tests involve placing a shovel blade flat atop the column and thumping on it harder and harder with a fist. There's even a "burp" test, in which a skier positions a small column of snow against his shoulder and taps it with the underside of a shovel.

As Deschenes was well aware, snowpits have their limitations. They provide a peek at the layering beneath the surface, but only at one particular spot. The snowpack can vary tremendously across a slope (the manuals call it "spatial variability") due to factors such as elevation and slope aspect. Although snowpit tests at well-chosen sites reveal useful information, numerous avalanches have been triggered at weak points only meters from where a test result indicated more stable conditions. Predicting snow stability is like forecasting the weather, with a huge number of variables that can affect the outcome. The devil is in the details.

Deschenes knew that, on top of all that information, he'd have to use his own intuition. Seasoned observers have a "seat of the pants" feeling about certain snow conditions. When you've seen avalanches happen in those conditions, you might decide to back off, no matter what the tests you are conducting say. Even for the experts, backcountry skiing carries a degree of risk and uncertainty.

On December 23, three members of Deschenes's group were carving turns down a slope in an area known as Grizzly Bowl, creating three sets of side-by-side slalom tracks. The middle skier fell, and the jolt was apparently enough to trigger a slide about 75 meters away on a steeper, 45-degree slope. This was the same area where a 1990 avalanche had fatally buried a father and son. This time, luckily, all the skiers were safely beyond reach. They watched, wide-eyed, as a fracture line split the snow and the slope below it released, the avalanche sliding on a layer of faceted crystals right at ground level. The group recorded the slide as 60 meters across with a slab depth of 50 to 150 centimeters at the crown. As one of them reported in the Slocan Chief logbook, "Yikes!"

DURING THAT SAME period over Christmas, Sean McTague was staying at the other cabin in Kokanee Glacier Park, Silver Spray. The first group of paying clients, Driscoll's group,

41

wasn't due until the following week, and McTague, as one of the hut custodians, had flown up to make sure the cabin was shoveled out and ready. He'd been joined there by his sister and some friends.

The clear, cold weather gave McTague and his group magnificent sunrises and sunsets, bathing the peaks in rosy hues. Sirius shone incredibly bright in the sky during their nighttime jaunts to the outhouse. The surroundings at the Silver Spray cabin were breathtaking, but the instability in the snowpack was spooky. One member of McTague's group did a slope test that scored so low it prompted them all to abandon skiing and return to the cabin for some tobogganing in a safe area. On Christmas Eve, a small avalanche came down just outside the cabin. There were fewer gentle, well-treed slopes around Silver Spray to ski in times of potential avalanche hazard. McTague himself hadn't bothered skiing the whole time he was there; he had plenty of cleaning up and shoveling to do.

Both McTague's group at Silver Spray and Deschenes's group at the Slocan Chief flew back to Kootenay Lake on December 27 to make room for the new groups flying in that day: the party of skiers from Utah to the Slocan Chief cabin, and Rob Driscoll's party of six, plus their cabin custodian, Lise Nicola, to Silver Spray.

The weaknesses within the snowpack at both places were evident, but so far there hadn't been enough additional load to cause major slab avalanches to release on the slopes. There had been no new snow all week.

"It was almost as if conditions weren't quite prime yet," Marc Deschenes would recall. "But in the backs of our minds, with the next snow load, the next storm, things were going to deteriorate even more." He thought it was fortunate that a lot of heli-ski operators, including the company he worked for, hadn't officially begun operations yet. "'Cause I tell you, it would have been stressful out there."

{4}

SNOW SLEUTHS

SNOW IS A RIDDLE, a transitory substance that's hard to get a fix on. Scientists call it a "multiscale phenomenon," meaning that the snow's composition at any one time is a result of the complex interactions of many factors, from weather conditions during its initial earthbound tumble to subsequent recrystallization within the snowpack. Snow's mutating structure and infinite variability are enough to make an avalanche forecaster's head spin. As Bob Brown, who studied avalanches for thirty years at Montana State University, told *Wired* magazine in 2003, "When I worked on the Apollo space program, I thought rocket science was the hardest form of physics, but snow science is even harder . . ."

Some of the scientists who probe the mysteries of snow torrents chose the field after their interest was piqued by a near-death experience with one. But like those who track tornadoes or rare butterflies, most people who study avalanches don't often get a chance to see them in action. Even when they do get a first-hand look, the show is over in seconds.

The Swiss were the first to scientifically probe the avalanche phenomenon, which isn't surprising. Almost two-thirds of the country's mountain roads wind through avalanche terrain, and millions of people live in settlements in the mountains. Avalanches in the European Alps have claimed thousands of victims over the years, one of the first recorded incidents being when Hannibal lost about eighteen thousand men, plus horses and elephants, while crossing the Alps to battle the Roman army in 218 BC. Once residents of the Alps starting building their villages high in the mountains, they, too, learned the hard way where the avalanches ran. The worst of many catastrophes was the Rodi avalanche in 1618, which buried the town of Plurs, Switzerland, killing over two thousand people.

The Swiss Federal Institute for Snow and Avalanche Research in Davos began operations in 1942, boosting its efforts after the particularly deadly winter of 1951, when ninety-one avalanche deaths were recorded in Switzerland alone. Today, the Swiss Institute remains a powerhouse of research and activity, and the Swiss have exported their expertise—and their experts—worldwide.

In France, which joins Switzerland at the forefront of avalanche studies, the catastrophic avalanche winter of 1970 (including a slide at Val d'Isere that killed thirty-nine children), spurred the founding of the French Association for Snow and Ice Study (ANENA) in Grenoble. The institute coordinates the work of various research agencies and provides education and training. Countries such as Norway, Austria, Italy, Iceland, Russia and Japan have also established varying levels of avalanche research.

The beginnings of North American scientific engagement with avalanches dates to December 27, 1946. "That night, I declared personal war against avalanches," writes Monty Atwater, the larger-than-life pioneer of avalanche research in the United States, in his colorful memoir *The Avalanche Hunters*. Atwater had been a member of the 10th Mountain Division, ski troops trained for high-elevation fighting during the Second World War. His practical experience had snared him a postwar job with the U.S. Forest Service, keeping avalanches at bay at a new ski resort in Utah. The Alta ski area featured 12,000-foot peaks, huge snowfalls and a bad rap sheet of destructive avalanches. Two days after Christmas 1946, another torrent of snow swept down on three high-school boys. They had been camping out at an abandoned mining shack and were skiing across a steep slope in a blizzard when the avalanche hit, completely burying one of them. "What followed was the most nightmarish experience of my life," writes Atwater. A ragtag band of rescuers from the ski resort, "lift operators, desk clerks, cooks, chambermaids, old men, young girls," struggled 300 meters up the mountain through waist-deep snow to help. Luckily, they were able to dig out the boy, who was conscious but badly injured. Strapping him to his own skis to form a makeshift stretcher, they brought him down the mountain in the dark on a succession of shoulders. After this accident, Atwater set out to learn all he could about avalanches.

The Swiss had been coming up with ways to protect their towns, roads and railways for years, but Atwater was more concerned with saving lives on the ski hill. He was one of the first on this side of the Atlantic to actively seek out avalanches and experiment with preemptively triggering slides that might otherwise catch skiers by surprise. At first he set off these avalanches himself, by simply skiing across the loaded slopes. Then, borrowing from the Swiss, he experimented with explosives, a job rife with occupational hazards. Avalanche control with explosives is now standard procedure, but it was a novel concept in the 1940s. Atwater describes climbing right up the avalanche path to place charges in the starting zone, narrowly escaping becoming an avalanche statistic himself more than once. "No one ever had so much fun hunting avalanches as we did, or ever will again," he wrote about those early days. Later, avalanche hunters discovered they could deliver the punch from a safer distance by using artillery.

The 1951–52 "Winter of the Big Snow" confirmed that these efforts were working. Although uncontrolled slides wreaked havoc elsewhere, the Alta area was unscathed, as were two other locations in the United States that had avalanche control, Berthoud Pass in Colorado and Stephens Pass in the Cascades of Washington State. At the end of that winter, Atwater wrote the first comprehensive manual of avalanche forecasting and control, *The Forest Service Avalanche Handbook*. In updated and revised editions, *The Avalanche Handbook* is still the North American bible.

During the 1960 Winter Olympics held at Squaw Valley, California, Atwater was given the job of keeping the slopes safe. This he accomplished by blasting them with recoilless rifles early and often. His Alta headquarters became a major center for avalanche research, and he was joined there by others, such as Ed LaChapelle and Ron Perla, who would become pre-eminent in the field. Later, the research headquarters was moved from Alta to the Rocky Mountain Experimental Station. Those were the golden years of avalanche research in the United States. Then the ax fell. Funding dried up during the 1980s, and research at the station was phased out, leaving American avalanche researchers scrabbling for funds. But advances continued to be made in countries such as Canada.

The Canadian story starts in the 1950s at Rogers Pass, the precipitous niche through British Columbia's Selkirk Mountains. The railway through there had long since retreated into underground tunnels, but plans were afoot for construction of a trans-Canada highway, a vital transportation link that would be routed through the pass. This time, planners decided they needed to get a better handle on the avalanches pummeling the route.

Canada's pioneer snow guy was Noel Gardner, a Glacier Park warden. Magazine accounts of his achievements describe him as demanding, headstrong and physically tough—a true mountain man. He was also a dedicated, committed researcher who "thought snow twenty-four hours a day," according to a quote from colleague Art Judson, a snow ranger with the U.S. Forest Service at the time. Gardner made regular surveys on skis through Rogers Pass to document the location, frequency and size of avalanches. Building on work done by Atwater, he started to develop a system for integrating snow profiles with weather patterns to predict when those slides would run. Canada's National Research Council became interested in Gardner and provided funds for a research station and field staff. The NRC wanted data about slide occurrence and dynamics so that the industrial infrastructure then being constructed in the western mountains—highways, railroads, and hydroelectric transmission towers—could be built to withstand snow torrents. The ground-breaking work done by Gardner at Rogers Pass included the design of a system for field record-keeping and formalized observations that provides researchers today with over forty years of consistent records. Monty Atwater was one of many experts from other countries who came to check out what was happening at

Gardner's Avalanche Research Centre. He later wrote about the "painful" contrast between what the Canadians were doing and the situation in the United States at the time.

Swiss civil engineer Peter Schaerer was hired by Canada's National Research Council in the 1950s to engineer the avalanche defense structures along the new highway. When the Trans-Canada Highway was finally completed through Rogers Pass in 1962, the defense system included earth barriers, snow sheds protecting vulnerable stretches of road, and artillery positions from which to shoot down hanging snow on the more than 140 avalanche paths threatening the highway. Schaerer continued to play an important role in the development of avalanche expertise in Canada, helping to lay the groundwork for the Canadian Avalanche Association in the early 1980s. A decade later, when the National Research Council cut back funding for avalanche research—money was short and many of the NRC's original questions had been answered—the association received short-term support to establish a nonprofit, national avalanche agency to coordinate all avalanche programs—the Canadian Avalanche Centre. Canada's centralized approach, reflecting the CAC's origins as a federally funded agency, is very different from the way things have evolved in the western United States, where over a dozen separate, locally based avalanche centers, most under the auspices of the U.S. Forest Service, operate more or less autonomously. The Canadian model has made it easier for those north of the border to move ahead in the areas of avalanche certification, standardized avalanche courses, and coordinated education and awareness programs.

After governments slashed their support for research, North American academic institutions picked up some of the slack. Canada's research efforts are centered at the University of Calgary and the University of British Columbia in Vancouver. Many of the people currently working in the American avalanche scene graduated from Montana State University, and there are also research programs at campuses in Colorado, Wyoming and California.

Snow is amazing stuff, and scientists spend lifetimes trying to fathom its properties. "To me, the mystery has never been that [snow] avalanches but that it usually stays on the mountain so well," wrote Monty Atwater in his memoir. Snow sleuths, wherever they may be, are constantly assembling clues about when, where, why and how snow falls off the mountain. For example, what exactly initiates an avalanche? What factors contribute to tipping the balance on an unstable slope? What part is played by hard and soft slabs, or thin or thick facet layers? What determines how fast and how far an avalanche will travel?

It's tricky getting into the thick of an avalanche, but intrepid Montana State researchers have positioned themselves inside an instrument-filled shack right in the firing line, then triggered an avalanche so that they could monitor the transformation of the snowpack, from settled mass to raging torrent to ice-hard debris. Swiss researchers have constructed a 30-meter-long snow slide equipped with radar detectors and other instruments to measure avalanches in action. The country has a research valley where they can trigger avalanches with explosives and measure them every which way. A wind tunnel is used to study the wind transport of snow.

Some researchers are attempting to turn the snowpack into a mathematical model, developing computer simulations of slab failures and avalanche flow. But it's no simple matter to convert snow stability into numbers, according to Mark Mueller, executive director of the American Avalanche Association. "When we look at computer programs that will forecast avalanche probability, we know parameters regarding terrain, we can model the weather and its impact, but the ability of snow structure to support the stress that's been added to it—that's the hard part, the part that's probably least understood."

In North America, much of the research focuses on this issue of snow stability. In this part of the world, we protect avalanche-threatened highways by detonating explosives to dislodge dangerously unstable snow. So we need to know when the snow is going to stay on the mountain and when it is ready to slide. What's the right time for the pre-emptive bombing strike?

In Europe, where explosives are reserved for use at ski resorts, highways and settlements are protected with physical barriers and strict land-use restrictions. Maps identify "red zones," where no houses can be constructed, or "yellow zones," where restrictions apply. European research concentrates more on avalanche dynamics and flow. What forces do structures such as cones, fences or tunnels have to withstand? How far could a one-in-fifty-year avalanche event flow?

One of several innovative avenues of research in North America involves using sensors to detect the infrasonic waves generated by avalanches many kilometers away. These waves, which resonate well below the level of human hearing, are also produced by nuclear explosions, earthquakes and volcanoes. Sensors can pick up the distinctive, infrasonic "voiceprint" of an avalanche, allowing researchers to gather information on the incidence of slides in the backcountry and the conditions under which unseen avalanches flow. Another avenue of research uses CAT scans to probe the inner mysteries of the snowpack.

Yet despite decades of research and the application of some very sophisticated technology, avalanches are still somewhat of an enigma. Snow is a complex material, and avalanche prediction an imperfect science. As veteran avalanche expert Ron Perla has written, "When it comes to judging slope stability, the first rule of thumb is that there are no rules of thumb."

{5}

RISKY BUSINESS

*

N HIS SMALL, crowded office at the Canadian Avalanche
Centre, Evan Manners was glued to the phone. He was
consulting with his network of experts to get their read on
snow conditions and potential hazards, so that his next public
avalanche bulletin, to be issued December 29, would reflect
their years of experience. The center issued four separate avalanche bulletins (since increased to five) twice a week (now
three times), describing snowpack conditions in the mountain
regions that together encompassed slopes from the Rocky
Mountains to the Pacific coast.

Manners has spent most of his working life dealing with
avalanches, first as a Parks Canada warden participating
in winter rescues, then while controlling snow slides along
Alberta's spectacular Banff-Jasper highway. Since 1996, he
has managed the day-to-day operations of the Canadian
Avalanche Centre, the hub of avalanche information, education and training in western Canada. From there, Manners

has his finger on the pulse of the avalanche situation. Every day during avalanche season, a stream of snow profile data, field observations and avalanche sightings pours into the office via computer, phone and fax.

The CAC's storefront office is located in Revelstoke, British Columbia, a small town tucked between the Selkirk and Monashee ranges of the Columbia Mountains, 160 kilometers north of Kokanee Glacier Park. The Trans-Canada Highway zooms right by the town, heading east towards Rogers Pass. Revelstoke is an old railway center, dating from the 1880s, and it still is a major point for tracking, dispatch and train crew changes. More recently, this community of nine thousand people has become a destination for snow sports. In winter, when walls of snow line the sidewalks (Revelstoke's website claims an average annual snowfall of over 18 meters), the town's hotels swarm with heli-skiers and sledders.

The avalanche center was established here in 1991 by the Canadian Avalanche Association, a body of professionals dedicated to deepening their understanding of avalanches, encouraging communication among their members, promoting avalanche industry standards and providing avalanche training. The stateside equivalent is the American Avalanche Association. The handful of staff working in the Canadian office are kept busy coordinating a wide range of activities, but underlying everything is the ongoing quest to learn more about this conundrum of snow falling off mountain slopes. As Evan Manners had discovered, avalanches provide a never-ending learning challenge.

Much of the information used to prepare the CAC's public bulletins came from the center's daily industry information exchange, a program key to the center's operations since its

54

inception. The idea grew out of coroners' recommendations following two commercial heli-skiing deaths that happened shortly before the center opened. In each case, investigators discovered that there had been a similar avalanche incident in the area shortly before the fatal occurrence. These incidents could have served as early warnings of increased avalanche hazard, but who knew about them? Both coroners recommended that the industry build some kind of communications network—an information exchange among neighbors near and far.

The CAC went boldly forth with a rudimentary computer system and an initial network of about thirty members. Eventually, the Information Exchange (Info-Ex) expanded to include most of the province's major heli-ski companies, ski resort operators, national parks, highway avalanche control programs and snow scientists. These front-line professionals send in daily observations to the avalanche center about weather, snowpack and avalanche occurrence in their regions. The information is summarized overnight and distributed confidentially to other members of the network. (The cooperative nature of this exchange, despite the fact that many of its members are commercial competitors, has impressed other countries attempting to set up coordinated approaches to avalanche prevention.)

Information from the industry exchange not only benefits its members but also provides an excellent data stream for the public avalanche bulletins that staff at the Canadian Avalanche Centre put together. To predict conditions in the mountains over the next few days, staff uses the information from the previous day's industry exchange in conjunction with the best available mountain weather forecast, as the weather could change things for better or for worse. They often go to the phones to consult further with the avalanche pros before releasing the bulletin.

Public avalanche bulletins are produced in many areas of the world. The Swiss began putting out hazard warnings in 1976 and now issue them daily, in three languages, for some twenty different mountain regions. France, Austria, Italy, Slovakia, Japan, Russia, New Zealand and the United States also issue regular warnings. (Scotland puts out bulletins, too, but they are aimed at climbers rather than skiers, Scottish skiing being what it is.) Many bulletins can be accessed by phone or online.

Most public bulletins include a scale to describe the level of avalanche danger, similar to the rating scale used for forest fire hazard. On the Canadian scale, the danger is categorized as Low (when natural avalanches or human-triggered avalanches are very unlikely), Moderate (natural avalanches unlikely; human-triggered avalanches *possible*), Considerable (natural avalanches possible; human-triggered avalanches *probable*), High (natural and human-triggered avalanches *likely*) or Extreme (widespread natural and human-triggered avalanches *certain*).

After years of debating the semantics, American avalanche forecasters adopted a similar five-level scale. Some had argued that the term "Considerable," falling between "Moderate" and "High," was ambiguous. Others felt that the scale took the wrong direction when it attempted to classify avalanche "danger," since the level of danger was, in part, dependent on human behavior in the backcountry. If people kept off the slopes, they argued, there was no danger at all. Instead, they suggested classifying snowpack in terms of "instability."

Some experts were wary of giving names to the ratings at all, since skiers often latched onto the labels without reading the full analysis of snow conditions or doing their own risk assessment. "The bulletin said 'Moderate,' so I didn't think the slope would avalanche" was the kind of oversimplification forecasters heard far too often.

Avalanches happen anywhere there are steep slopes and enough snow. But like the tree that falls in the forest when there's no one to hear it, most avalanches occur unnoticed, in remote areas. The ones that attract attention are those that endanger people.

At one time, humans stayed away from mountains. Mountains were the home of the gods, the lair of dragons and the domain of supernatural creatures. Even today, in some parts of the world, people living in the shadow of the peaks provide offerings to the mountain deities and avoid trespassing on their turf. Travelers, miners and other curious, greedy or intrepid souls eventually ventured into mountainous terrain, seeking the greener lands across the mountain passes or the minerals hidden in cracks and crannies of rock. It's only in the past century, however, that people have embraced North America's snowy winter mountains as their recreational playground.

Before the mid-1950s, the avalanches that injured or killed people in North America were largely industrial. Avalanches caused major headaches for those building the railways, highways, mines and hydroelectric transmission lines that opened up the West to economic development and settlement in the late 1800s and early 1900s. Miners toiling in the Colorado mountains were hit hard, with over one hundred avalanche fatalities during the bad winter of 1883–84. In April 1898, an avalanche on the Chilkoot Pass trail, gateway to Klondike gold, entombed more than sixty people in snow up to 10 meters deep.

Nineteen-ten goes down as the most devastating year in North American history for avalanche disasters. Two railway accidents, one in the United States and the other in Canada, were to blame. The American disaster happened along the Great Northern Railway line near Stephen's Pass, Washington, in the Cascade Mountains. A heavy February storm with high winds smothered the tracks with snow and avalanches, stopping all trains. At the tiny, one-hotel settlement of Wellington, passenger cars were pulled onto a parallel siding, where the passengers were stranded for six days while crews toiled to clear the tracks. Snow continued to build up on the treeless slopes above, which had recently been clearcut. Then the falling snow turned to rain. At 1:20 AM on March 1, a massive slide crashed down onto the tracks, sending railcars, locomotives and boxcars rolling into a ravine. Rescuers dug out twenty-two survivors, the last after eleven hours. They continued digging for a week, but the final body wasn't found until spring. Total death toll: ninety-six.

The avalanche north of the border that year, also in March, occurred on the transcontinental Canadian Pacific Railway route through Rogers Pass in the Selkirk Mountains. Railway builders had faced no end of challenges building a line through the pass, not the least of which was dealing with massive avalanches. In the days prior to March 4, over two meters of snow had fallen, followed by heavy rain and warm weather. The first large avalanche came down just west of Rogers Pass about 6:00 PM, burying the rail lines under seven meters of dense snow. A sixty-four-person crew was called in to clear the deposit, aided by a rotary snowplow attached to a locomotive. Around midnight, another large avalanche ran down the opposite slope, fatally burying sixty-two of the workers in the trench they had just dug. The fireman of the locomotive was luckier; he was sucked out of the window and thrown 30 meters onto an unused snow shed, sustaining internal injuries, a badly broken leg and a dislocated shoulder.

As mines began to close, and better zoning and workplace safety guidelines were put in place, the number of avalanche deaths dropped dramatically. But over the past few decades, the North American avalanche toll has been steadily rising again. The reason is the huge growth in the popularity of backcountry winter recreation—skiing, ski mountaineering, snowmobiling and snowboarding. More than three-quarters of all avalanche deaths in North America now involve people recreating, rather than working, on mountain slopes, a trend echoed elsewhere in the world. At first those fatalities included people downhill skiing at commercial ski hills, but now that avalanche control is as routine at most ski areas as groomed runs and liability releases, virtually all accidents occur out of bounds, where the mountains are still wild and the avalanches run free. Over the past few decades, more and more people have been ducking under the ropes or heading for the hills to play in this avalanche zone. Unfortunately, a small number also die there.

Bulletins are one way to inform the public about avalanche risk. Another is education. The Canadian Avalanche Association Training Schools, already providing courses for industry professionals, developed a standardized curriculum for avalanche courses offered to recreational backcountry skiers in 1996. The courses were subsequently tailored to suit the other sport groups that had started to show up in the statistics. Snowmobilers now have machines weighing a quarter tonne, with loads of power and traction that allow them to roar into terrain that was once beyond their reach. The practice of high-marking—riding a machine straight up a steep mountain slope to see how far it will go—is lethal on an unstable snowpack. Demographically, sledheads are predominantly male and middle-aged, with a high disposable income and some resistance to being lectured about safety precautions. The CAC usually approaches them at a family level. Instructors urge sledders to minimize their risks by, for example, reducing the number of machines on an avalanche-prone slope at any one time and keeping observers outside the track rather than within the run-out zone.

Snowboarders, too, have begun getting their own avalanche courses, geared not only to their different equipment but also to the younger demographic. These young folks are keen; they don't have a lot of money, but they're willing to learn about safety in the backcountry; and they aren't yet set in their ways. Some of the programs aimed at youth are designed to offset media images that glamorize taking inappropriate risks. But while some members of these other groups are learning the hard way about the dangers of the backcountry, and in the United States more snowmobilers are now killed each year by avalanches than skiers, in Canada, it is backcountry skiers who are most likely to be caught in an avalanche.

"The goal is zero tragedy but there will always be some," says Evan Manners. After his years in the business, he is able to tick off four stages in the development of avalanche risk awareness.

"The first stage would be you're so unaware of the risk you don't even realize you're at risk. It never occurs to you to worry about avalanches, and when one hits, it seems to have come out of the blue.

"The second stage is where you're aware that there's a danger you should be afraid of, but you don't know how to deal with it, you don't know what to do, and you're totally at the mercy of other people's help or advice.

"The third stage is where you are starting to learn enough about this phenomenon that you can begin to make judgments." This is a precarious stage, Manners points out; skiers can know just enough to feel confident, causing many to overestimate their avalanche skills, sometimes vastly. "And the fourth stage of learning is where you have enough experience and knowledge that risk avoidance becomes somewhat subconscious. A lifetime is probably an appropriate learning period for that."

{ 6 }

MOCK RESCUE

Saturday, December 27

ISE NICOLA strode across a well-trampled snow slope near the Silver Spray cabin, a 3-meter-long probe pole in her hand. While the skiers in Rob Driscoll's group unpacked in the cabin, Nicola was checking to see that everything was ready for the mock-avalanche rescue scenario. The procedure was outlined in the hut keeper's Operational Safety Guidelines, which also described the other duties she would be expected to perform during the week, such as monitoring the radio from 8:00 AM to 8:00 PM daily, relaying weather and avalanche forecasts, recording weather readings and snow stability observations, making sure the cabin was used properly, and keeping the outhouse clean.

Sean McTague's group had helped out by setting up the rescue scenario that morning while waiting for their helicopter to arrive. They had begun by digging four holes, up to a meter in depth, in the snow. Into each of these they had inserted a plastic bag containing a wallet-sized avalanche beacon. Several extra beacons were kept at the cabin for this purpose, and they also served as backups in case a client forgot to bring one. The group had set all the beacons on "send" mode before placing them in the snow, so that they would transmit radio signals. Then they had filled in the holes. Next, McTague and his friends had found a spot to dig a larger excavation, and into that trench they had placed a large stuffed bag. Once again, they covered over the evidence. And that was it: the five victims were in place on this pseudo-avalanche slope, ready to be found. McTague's group finished by tromping all over the slope, making it impossible to tell where they had dug the holes. Now, checking their work, Nicola poked her pole into the snow at the spot where they'd told her the stuffed bag was buried. After a few tries, her probe encountered something firm. Ah, there it was. She disguised the site of her probing with a few more bootprints before calling in the search party.

Back in the cabin, the skiers had been sorting their gear. When they headed out onto the slopes, each of them would be carrying a lightweight snow shovel with a telescoping shaft and detachable blade that fit inside their packs or could be strapped to the outside, as well as a collapsible avalanche probe like Nicola's: a long, thin metal rod, in six sections threaded by shock cord, that could be extended to three meters in length. At least one person in the group would need to bring a map and compass for navigating, as well as first aid supplies and a repair kit in case of broken bindings. Duct tape was always handy to have along. Sawing through the snow to dig a pit required a length of knotted cord, and those who were interested in the finer points of snowpack analysis would carry a kit containing a thermometer, a folding ruler, a crystal screen (a plastic card marked with a millimeter grid), a magnifying glass and a field book.

Everybody would pack a warm hat, mitts and extra clothing, goggles if it was snowing, sunglasses, a visor hat, and sunscreen and lip protection in case the skies cleared to blue. Even in January, sun reflecting off snow at that elevation can cause sunburn. A headlamp was advisable given the short days at this time of year, as well as overnight survival items such as matches and a lightweight emergency blanket or bivvy sack. Skin wax was helpful, since wet snow often sticks to a ski's climbing skin. A water bottle, of course, and food. Those would be the basic items. If the group decided to start out by skiing downhill rather than climbing, they would need to be sure their skins were folded up in their packs, too.

When Lise Nicola called the group outside for the mock avalanche rescue, each skier brought along an avalanche beacon, a shovel and a probe pole. Once they had assembled on the nearby slope, Nicola described the boundaries of the avalanche track that they should imagine lay before them. She then assumed her role of witness, acting disoriented and saying that five companions who had been skiing the slope with her had been swept away by a torrent of snow. The group sprang into action.

AVALANCHES ARE to the mountain skier what tidal rips and rogue waves are to the surfer at sea—they come with the territory. The less threatening kind of avalanche is called a sluff. When the snow near the surface of the snowpack is loose and unconsolidated, a sluff can start from a single point, collecting more snow as it moves and widening into a triangular shape.

More often, though, the snowpack operates as a cohesive mass held together by millions of tiny ice connections. Gravity pulls the entire mass downwards, causing the top section to shear off in a single slab at a weak layer within the snowpack. The slab slides over the bottom portion of the snowpack like the top layer of a cake sliding on soft icing, or a sandwich shearing at the mayo. In these cases, it usually turns out that the snowpack has come apart at a buried plane of loose crystals poorly bonded to the snow layers above or below. This is a slab avalanche, the kind that usually kills backcountry skiers.

Every slab avalanche is initiated at a start zone—somewhere the snow, under extreme stress, is poised to release. A sudden extra load or a vibration triggers the collapse, and the avalanche begins to run. An avalanche can be triggered naturally; by a chunk of snow falling off an overhanging cornice, for instance, or by a concentrated heavy fall of snow or rain. But in 95 per cent of avalanche accidents that involve people, it's the weight of the victims themselves, or their companions, that actually triggers the slide.

Once on the move, an avalanche breaks into blocks that continue to accelerate, scooping up snow ahead of them. Some of the snow may become airborne, flowing in a billowing powder cloud above the denser torrent. Within five seconds a big avalanche can be smoking down a slope at 50 kilometers an hour, and it continues to accelerate, reaching speeds as high as 200 kilometers an hour. An air blast, pushed out in front by the rapidly moving snow, precedes the slide.

In avalanche lingo, the top of the slide, where the slab breaks away from the upper slope, is called the crown. Along the sides of the avalanche are the flanks. The path the slide runs down is called the track, and the bottom, where the snow spills out onto the flat, loses momentum and stops, successive waves of snow piling up from behind, is the run-out zone or the toe.

In Canada, slides are given a ranking between one and five. A size one avalanche, with a typical mass of 10 tonnes, is relatively harmless to people. Yet even a negligible slide can be treacherous if it sweeps skiers over cliffs or into gullies. A size three, with a mass of 1000 tonnes, can bury a car, rip apart a small building or break trees. The chances of a person surviving an avalanche of this size are slim. The largest avalanches, size five, have a mass of 100,000 tonnes and the power to destroy an entire village or a 40-hectare forest. The American avalanche classification system is slightly different, based on the volume of snow tumbling down relative to the size of the historic avalanche path. The same volume of snow may classify as a small or a large avalanche, depending on the size of the slides that have preceded it.

All of the groups staying at the Silver Spray and Slocan Chief cabins have started their week with an avalanche rescue exercise. The routine was implemented after the avalanche that buried a father and his adult son, both locals, while they were skiing at the Slocan Chief in 1990. Cabin custodians had also discovered over the years that every group seemed to include someone who had a malfunctioning avalanche beacon, or didn't know how to operate the beacon properly. Different brands of beacons have different bells and whistles. Clients coming to the cabin brought their own equipment, and they didn't always understand how to work the beacons they had just rented or bought. It's not enough for a skier to wear a transmitting avalanche beacon, either, unless she is sure that she is the one who will be buried. To be any use at finding companions buried under tonnes of avalanche debris, she also needs to be efficient at doing a search. Even for experienced searchers, practices are never a waste of time, and few recreationalists have done enough test runs to be able to locate a body in time to save a life.

Several of the people in Rob Driscoll's group had avalanche training and experience with beacon searches, so they immediately set to work. The most important survival factor in an avalanche rescue is how long it takes to recover the victims. With no time for committee discussions, someone has to take charge, assign tasks and coordinate the search efforts. Pat Von Blumen took on the lead role.

First, Von Blumen did a visual check of the slopes above the slide path to be sure the path was safe from further avalanches. Was there hanging snow that hadn't released with the original slide but might still come down on the searchers? (Rule number one: Don't bring more victims to the accident.)

Next, he asked Nicola to point out the spot where she had last seen the victims. That would narrow down the potential search area, since victims wouldn't be buried above that point. Their bodies would likely be somewhere down the fall line, probably at a spot where the snow deposit was deeper than elsewhere. A human body is about three times as dense as avalanche debris, so it tends to sink as an avalanche slows its descent, even briefly, due to fluctuations in the terrain.

Von Blumen ordered the searchers to switch their beacons from send mode to receive mode, so they'd be ready to pick up radio signals from the buried victims. Avalanche beacons, also called transceivers, are low-power electromagnetic devices that are normally strapped to the body under outer clothing. Most are powered by small AA batteries. While out skiing, each wearer has his beacon in the "send" position. That way, he will be transmitting continuous beeping signals that can be picked up by anyone else in range whose beacon is set to "receive."

Once a skier is buried by a slide, the best hope of finding him quickly is to hone in on the signal transmitting from his beacon beneath the snow. Many models of beacon augment the audio function with a visual display—a line of little lights that flash, first one, then the next, and eventually all of them, as the searcher moves closer to the source. All beacons now transmit at the international standard frequency of 457 kilohertz. At the beginning of each skiing day, one person in the party normally turns his beacon to "receive" to make sure that he can pick up signals from everyone else, confirming that all the beacons are functioning.

Von Blumen told the other searchers to assemble their shovels while he sent one person onto the avalanche track to do a hasty search. The single searcher raced in a zigzag pattern over potential burial areas, beacon in hand, with the volume set to maximum to detect any signals. He also checked for clues on the surface of the slide path, hats or gloves that would indicate a line of flow and help determine high probability areas for burials. Heavy boots make running a challenge on an uneven snowfield, but Nicola's watch was recording each passing second. Each time a beep was detected, the single searcher called out, and Von Blumen dispatched a second person to zero in on the source while the first one continued looking for further signals. Usually one person is assigned to zero in on each victim; if too many people become involved, they hear beeping from each other's beacons and get confused.

Moving quickly, yet trying to be careful and accurate, each secondary searcher turned down his or her beacon's volume to better gauge where a signal became louder or softer, trying to pinpoint its exact source. Some searchers prefer the traditional grid method, moving in one direction until they detect the loudest signal, then turning down their volume control and searching at right angles from that point. They repeat this until, at the lowest volume setting, they're right over the spot where the beeping is loudest. Others use a search method known as the induction method. Because the signal is strongest along the lines of electromagnetic force that arc around the transmitting beacon (in the same pattern formed by iron filings on paper when a magnet is placed underneath), a searcher who has located a signal can follow it along a curving path that will lead to the source.

About five minutes had passed since the search began. Whenever a signal was pinpointed, the searchers would probe the spot to feel for the beacon or simply grab a shovel and dig for the buried plastic bag. After a beacon was retrieved, it was turned off so that its signal wouldn't interfere with the ongoing search for other "victims." In a real rescue situation, searchers would uncover the buried victim's head, clear her nose and mouth, and ideally have the skills to begin artificial respiration or CPR as required. Most serious outdoors people are well versed in backcountry skills including first aid, and the cabin custodians in Kokanee Glacier Park were also expected to have up-to-date first aid training in addition to their avalanche certification.

Driscoll and the other searchers recovered the four beacons, but they were baffled about the lack of a signal from the fifth "body." Where was that person? Maybe the fifth victim hadn't been wearing a beacon, or the beacon wasn't transmitting for some reason. Von Blumen initiated a probe search.

"Carry a probe as you would have others do for you" is one of avalanche veteran Ron Perla's rules of thumb, and most well-equipped backcountry skiers do. A regular ski pole with

69

the basket removed is better than nothing, but nowhere as effective.

One avalanche rescue manual describes a probe search as "a miserable, cold, long and desperate exercise." Compared to a transceiver search, it is painfully slow, and it is usually used as a last resort. Most victims wearing avalanche beacons can be located by their signals in five to fifteen minutes, if the search is efficient. Digging them out of avalanche debris can take as long or longer, because the air has been pounded out of the snow, making it as hard as rock. When a probe search is required, it will take five probers about one hundred times as long to find a buried victim as it will one searcher with a transceiver.

Driscoll and his friends first spot-probed in areas upslope of trees, rocks or obstacles where snow and other debris might accumulate. To more systematically search the broad area, they formed a probe line. Lined up side by side, they moved in unison up the avalanche track. With each step forward, they pushed their probes down into the snow, punching out a grid search pattern. The space between individuals determines whether searchers are doing a coarse probe or a fine one. They are feeling for a body. But even with a probe line, there is a chance that the body will be missed, particularly if it was buried more or less upright.

Eventually one of Driscoll's group encountered something soft yet resistant under the snow. Leaving the probe in place, he dug to investigate, recovering the stuffed bag representing the final buried body. All of the missing skiers were now accounted for.

Lise Nicola's manual suggested that she follow the mock search with a short discussion to answer questions and reinforce important points. She emphasized that the group was responsible for its own safety. Her job was to maintain the cabin, pass on weather reports and avalanche bulletins, and, in the event of an emergency, operate the radio and act as dispatcher. Even when she went skiing with them (she wasn't permitted to ski on her own), she would not be acting in the role of a guide. Clients were totally responsible for themselves when it came to route selection and self-rescue. During previous stints as hut keeper, Nicola had often declined to go out skiing with clients, because she didn't trust their judgment or level of expertise. She thought much more highly of this group, some of whom had extensive backcountry experience and avalanche training.

"Is everyone now confident in their ability to deal with an actual avalanche self-rescue situation?" That was the closing question of the mock rescue session. Less experienced members of the group were encouraged to keep practicing, and all were reminded that they should perform snow stability tests before entering avalanche terrain. Nicola urged them to think ahead by constantly asking themselves, "What if?" and "Then what?" Even in the case of an emergency, outside help would take over two hours to arrive.

Rob Driscoll and his party knew the value of practicing avalanche rescues, and they also knew the bald truth: no matter how dazzling their rescue skills, their companions could be dead before the avalanche stopped moving, having slammed into rocks and trees on the descent or been swept over cliffs while rolling and tumbling out of control. The commonly cited statistic is that 25 per cent of avalanche victims die from injuries received on the way down. An additional 25 per cent die within thirty minutes of burial. Most buried victims survive

71

the first fifteen minutes, but after that survival rates plummet. Time is the enemy. A victim's best chance for survival depends on a speedy, effective search by well-equipped, knowledgeable companions. For victims buried more than two meters down, the survival rate is almost nil.

The avalanche rescue completed, Nicola led the group back to the cabin, so that they could finish the orientation there. While the search was unfolding, clouds had moved up the mountain, and visibility had deteriorated. Inside the cabin it was cozy, however, warmed by the wood stove. Leaving their boots just inside the door, the skiers hung their parkas on the short lengths of doweling that served as coat hooks and placed their damp mitts on the drying rack suspended above the stove. They settled on the benches on either side of the table and turned their attention back to Nicola.

She might be petite and soft-spoken, but Nicola communicated with easy confidence and authority as she ran through the routines. Guys were often impressed, and somewhat daunted, by this capable woman with a mass of dark curls who seemed to have her feet so firmly on the ground. She had the group list their names, along with the names and phone numbers of people to be contacted in an emergency. She encouraged them to write out their planned itinerary each day they skied, so if someone went missing, searchers would know where to start looking. She showed them how to operate the cabin's radio in case she wasn't able to do it, and pointed out the fire extinguishers. Housekeeping instructions covered such matters as sorting garbage, keeping food safe from martens and rodents by storing it in the lockable plastic bins outside, and not letting solids go down the drain in the sink, since they would clog the pipes. Water was carried in buckets from a hole punched through the ice on a creek close by. The outhouse was beyond that along a shoveled path, perched high above the ground on a wooden base. As several members of the group had already discovered, it had one of the best views from any outhouse anywhere, looking south on the panorama of snowy peaks and glaciers. Only a fool would close the door.

With the preliminaries completed, the group was now free to ski. But when they headed out that afternoon, the skiing left lots to be desired. There hadn't been any significant new snow in Kokanee Glacier Park for a week. The snowpack was still relatively thin, leaving the rocky slopes "bony." The snow surface was variable, often crusty, blown by wind into slabs and drifts. Sometimes, while carving turns, the skiers punched down through this crust into an underlying layer of loose crystals. The weather wasn't anything to write home about either, given the flat light and poor visibility.

There is no such thing as a bad day of skiing, but some days are definitely more memorable than others. And unless conditions improved, this ski week would be a bit of a bust. But it was only the first afternoon, and with any luck the mountain gods would cough up some fresh snow. In fact, the forecast called for a storm cycle to blow in over the next few days.

Back at home base, Driscoll and his cohorts hauled water, stoked the heater with wood and helped Nicola with her custodial chores. A gorgeous sunset, which the group watched from the helicopter pad, bathed the broken clouds and snowy peaks in glowing pink. In the fading light inside the cabin, they lit the propane lamps, poured the wine and prepared to spend their first night on the mountain.

{7}

THE PURSUIT OF POWDER

*

SKIING AS A MEANS of travel has been around for centuries. An ancient ski pulled from a Swedish peat bog has been pollen-dated to 2500 BC. Prehistoric rock carvings discovered along the coast of Norway and in caves in eastern Russia depict hunters on skis. Even the Norse winter goddess Skadi, after whom Scandinavia was named, was a skier. According to Norse mythology, Skadi dwelt high in the mountains. After an incompatible marriage to the sea god Njord, she replaced him with Ullr, god of skis, who shared her snow-going lifestyle. Ullr was such an impressive skier that he would streak across the sky, leaving the brilliant stars as his trails.

Norway is given credit for the birth of modern skiing, but the skis used there in the early 1800s looked very different from those used to shred powder today. They were 3 meters long with a simple toe strap. To brake or steer, skiers used a long stick or staff they could jam in the snow beside them or between their legs.

Farmers from the Telemark region of Norway took skiing a quantum leap forward, adding a heel strap of tough, elastic birch-root tendrils and inventing swooping telemark and skidded Christiania turns (precursors to Stem Christie turns). Then came the first sidecut ski—a ski shaped to be narrower at the waist and broader at tip and tail, allowing it to flex and therefore carve better turns. By the 1880s, the telemark skis turned out by Norwegian factories were being exported throughout Europe.

During the last half of the 1800s, many Scandinavians brought their passion for skiing across the Atlantic. Legendary John "Snowshoe" Thomson, who emigrated to the United States from Telemark, used skis for his overland mail run across the Sierra Nevadas, a 300-kilometer, five-day return trip that he made regularly between 1856 and 1876.

The sport of mountaineering had developed in Europe as a challenging, leisure pursuit for the physically fit and the well-to-do. Mountaineers discovered that skis could provide four-season access to the peaks, and ski expeditions were launched into the alpine of central Europe and Russia. They gained impetus with Norwegian hero Fridtkof Nansen's account of his trip on skis across the mid-Greenland ice cap, *On Skis over Greenland*, published in 1890.

Around the same time, the Canadian Pacific Railway brought some Swiss mountain guides to Canada to promote tourism at its Rocky Mountain hotels such as at Lake Louise. Some of these guides stayed for the winter, introducing the locals to skiing. Soon experienced skiers were embarking on long adventures in the Rocky Mountain backcountry, and ski mountaineering spread through other mountainous regions of western North America.

75

In the winter of 1929, a hydrologist and photographer named Orland Bartholomew made an audacious solo ski expedition, covering hundreds of kilometers, along the High Sierra mountains. His custom-made hickory skis were radically shorter and wider than other skis of the time; his poles were made from rake handles. Bartholomew's one-hundred-day trip from Lone Pine to Yosemite Valley, including avalanche encounters and a climb up 14,495-foot Mount Whitney en route, is still considered one of North America's great mountaineering adventures.

But the best part of this new winter sport, as far as many skiers were concerned, was the downhill run. People would spend all morning side-stepping up slopes just to ski down them again, so it was only a matter of time before entrepreneurs started building mechanized lifts. Continental holidays at ski resorts in the Alps were de rigueur by the 1920s, and North America's first purpose-built ski resorts appeared in the 1930s at Sun Valley, Aspen, Vail and Mammoth. A chairlift constructed from mining hoist parts opened at Alta, Utah, in 1938. Canada's first chairlift opened at Mount Tremblant, Quebec, that same year.

At the start of World War II, the outnumbered Finns donned skis and white clothing to mount a surprisingly effective resistance against the invading Soviet Union's Red Army. Their success piqued the interest of American military planners, and many of the U.S.'s best skiers and mountaineers joined the 10th Mountain Division, training on Mount Rainier and in the Colorado Rockies, carrying on war games at 13,000 feet. When they returned from the war, many of these veterans became ski instructors at the new downhill resorts.

Crowds began flocking to these groomed runs, spawning advances in ski equipment. Already, improved bindings were more effectively securing boot to ski, making it easier to torque downhill turns. In a fall, however, the skis stayed attached until the leg fractured, prompting the development of releasable bindings. Skis themselves morphed from straight boards to shaped boards, and from wood to aluminium, fiberglass and all manner of laminated construction materials, seeking the perfect combination of strength and flexibility.

During the 1970s, helicopter skiing was introduced into North America as the ultimate powder experience for those with sufficient money and stamina. A chopper whisked skiers to the top of the untracked runs. The less glamorous alternative was snowcat skiing, where a treaded snow machine did the same. The downhill scene was also turning off some nature lovers, who sought out quieter, less mechanized skiing possibilities. One result was a resurgence of Nordic skiing and a demand for cross-country ski trails. Others took up ski touring, heading deep into the mountains under their own steam, seeking unpatrolled, uncontrolled and untracked powder slopes.

There are two styles of backcountry ski touring, each with its own equipment. Telemark skiers use bindings that allow the boot heel to lift, so that skiers can perform graceful, bent-knee, free-heel turns. Alpine touring bindings secure the heel firmly to the ski, giving skiers more control. (Touring bindings have a different setting that allows heel lifting for the uphill climb.) Which of these ski techniques is better is a matter of great debate and personal preference. At one time telemark equipment was lighter in weight than its alpine touring cousin, but that is no longer the case. Telemarking requires skiers to learn a new technique, but converts love the freedom of those swooping turns. Those turns put more strain on the knees, however, so middle-aged tele-skiers with aching joints tend to switch to touring skis.

People unfamiliar with backcountry skiing sometimes think the sport is all about bombing down steep, untracked powder slopes. Films and magazine ads that promote the culture of "extreme" sports show backcountry skiers and boarders pushing the limits. No boundaries, no fear—including footage of skiers and boarders riding down the mountain in the midst of an avalanche. Such images reinforce the view that those who venture into the winter backcountry are reckless, risk-taking yahoos. But 90 per cent of the time skiers are in the mountains, they are slogging uphill, using mohair or nylon climbing skins that adhere to their ski bases. In that way, the sport has more in common with hiking than with blasting down runs at a ski resort.

Commercially guided ski touring groups are led by a professional guide, who breaks the trail uphill and makes the decisions about which routes and runs are safe. The self-guided crowd makes its own route decisions. Backcountry skiing requires specialized skills: the ability to navigate with map and compass, to choose safe travel routes, to cope with all manner of weather and snow conditions, and to deal with wilderness rescues and medical emergencies. It's also very hard work.

Only a fraction of alpine skiers have swapped the lifts and amenities of the ski resort for the wider possibilities. However, the number increases every year, and in some areas the backcountry has become downright crowded. It can be hard to even find parking at favorite areas such as Rogers Pass, British Columbia, or Teton Pass, Wyoming. This growing popularity of the backcountry in winter is a phenomenon found around the globe, from the Alps of Europe to those of New Zealand and Japan. But the pursuit of wild mountain powder is not without inherent dangers, chief among them the risk of avalanches. The more skiers stream into the back-country, the higher the likelihood that someone will be in the path of a slide.

A LOT OF AVALANCHE fatalities can be linked to ignorance. In Canada, a survey of noncommercial avalanche accidents (accidents not involving a professional guide) between 1984 and 1996 showed that about 75 per cent of the victims weren't wearing avalanche beacons. Overall, however, statistics suggest that backcountry skiers are getting much better at decision-making in the mountains, and that the number of fatalities is actually going down, on a per capita basis. More people are taking avalanche awareness courses, wearing beacons while they ski in the backcountry, and carrying shovels. More people are checking public avalanche bulletins like those issued by the Canadian Avalanche Centre before they head out.

But educators across North America have also noticed something disturbing. A significant number of people who have gone through avalanche safety courses and have the necessary technical tools are still ending up in avalanches. Why do skiers who have the skills to recognize the hazards apparently misread or ignore warning signs and ski into potential death traps? Increasingly, avalanche experts are zeroing in on human behavior for explanations.

"We make the right decisions about the conditions, and then we throw that out the window and do whatever we want," says Mark Mueller of the American Avalanche Association. "Unfortunately, that's all too common. What we see, when we look at and debrief some accidents, is that people who get caught see that conditions are favorable to avalanches, yet they get caught in them, anyway."

Avalanche educators have identified a long list of "perception traps," most of which will sound familiar to anyone who has toured on skis in the backcountry. For starters, if you really want to ski a slope, you are more likely to see the signs that indicate the slope is stable rather than those that suggest the opposite. Latching onto the piece of information that tells you what you want to hear, you may disregard other indications of avalanche hazard.

Skiers do this for many reasons. Maybe they've been stuck in a cabin for days because of bad weather and are desperate to get out onto the slopes. Or they've paid hundreds of bucks and taken time off work for a week of skiing heaven, and they don't want to miss out. Veteran avalanche educators Doug Fesler and Jill Fredston of the Alaska Mountain Safety Center call that "city thinking versus mountain thinking," and it affects a skier's ability to objectively focus on the mountain and what it is telling him or her.

"It applies to everybody across the board," says Mark Mueller. "It's the great equalizer between the experts and the novices. I have to check myself on it—that I'm not thinking, 'This can't happen to me because I'm an avalanche expert.' Well, sure it can happen to me. If I do something silly, if I'm motivated by the fact that it hasn't snowed for a long time, and I really want to ski some powder, and the only place there's any left is this place that's a little sketchy, but I think it's gonna be okay. . . . The avalanche isn't going to care whether I'm a beginner or an expert. It's just there, waiting."

Some faulty perceptions may be totally unconscious. Studies have shown that skiers think a sunny slope is friendlier than a shady one. When skies clear and the sun comes out after a storm, skiers instinctively feel that the danger is past. Yet the prime time for an avalanche accident is during or immediately after a storm. Most of them happen when the sky is blue.

Group dynamics also play a major role in the decisions people make on the slopes. The larger the group, the more boldly people tend to behave. But where avalanches are concerned, safety in numbers doesn't hold true: the added weight of a large group increases the risk of triggering a slide. In smaller groups, people tend to pay more attention to their surroundings. But in all cases, avalanche pros suggest, you should pretend to be alone as you ask yourself what risks you feel comfortable taking.

During a self-guided ski tour, it's common that the strongest skier in the group leads the way, breaking trail through deep snow. The rest tend to follow along. Unfortunately, the strongest skier, often an alpha male, won't necessarily make wise decisions or take into account the weaker members of the party. Those at the back of the pack may keep quiet despite their misgivings.

Ego, one-upmanship, a "go for it" mentality, pride, over-confidence and anger can all push people into risky territory. So can being excessively goal oriented, unwilling to turn around before reaching the day's objective. Late in the day, or when the weather craps out, there's a tendency to cut corners, to take shortcuts on the way back to the car or cabin, not to take sufficient time to properly evaluate the slopes. Some educators call this the "back to the barn" syndrome.

Psychologist and risk expert Gerald Wilde of Queens University in Kingston, Ontario, has introduced the avalanche community to a theory called risk homeostasis. The theory assumes that each person accepts a certain level of subjectively estimated risk when he or she participates in an activity such as backcountry skiing. Constantly checking the risk they are exposed to, people will take steps to reduce it if they feel the level is too high for them, perhaps by choosing a different route. But if the risk is lower than what they find acceptable, they will respond by increasing it—choosing steeper, more exposed slopes, for example. In other words, people continually adjust their actions to increase or reduce risk in order to maximize the benefits they get from the activity.

The theory challenges the idea that accidents are reduced by implementing more advanced safety measures. Instead, as people feel better protected by these safeguards, their perception of the inherent risk changes. In one startling study of the sport of skydiving, researchers discovered no decrease in the overall number of skydiving fatalities despite technical improvements that reduced the risk of parachutes not opening. Instead, as skydivers gained more confidence in their chutes, they waited until they were closer to the ground before pulling the cord, and the number of landing-related accidents increased. Avalanche educators wrestle with the thought that their students, by gaining a better understanding of the how and why of avalanches, might feel more confident going into marginal terrain. And they wonder if the new backcountry safety products just entering the market—including an avalung, a strap-on breathing tube attached to a snow filter, and an ABS (air bag system) backpack—might cause wearers to feel they can rachet up the risks they take.

According to Gerald Wilde, the key to reducing accidents is motivating people to alter the level of risk they are willing to incur. To improve traffic safety, for instance, agencies sometimes offer financial incentives such as lower insurance rates. But how to change the behavior of backcountry risk-takers is a question many avalanche educators ponder.

"Personally, I don't think you can," says the AAA's Mark Mueller, who has chewed over that issue a lot. Aggressive risk-takers frequently enroll in the courses Mueller teaches, and he knows they are going to get out there and push the envelope. "You can teach them how to travel in a way that enhances their margin of safety. But ultimately, people are going to make their own decisions. You can provide them with a little window on their decision-making and an opportunity to see where bad decisions have been made in the past, but you can't make these decisions for them."

The scientific definition of risk is the probability of an event multiplied by its harmful consequences. The trickiest risks to evaluate are those that have low probability but dangerous consequences. The probability of a commercial airliner crashing is very low, for example, but the consequences are generally fatal. The chances of being caught in a fatal avalanche are also very low. Usually, even when people ski on unstable snow in avalanche terrain, nothing occurs; they get away with it. That's why so many skiers are tempted. But fatal avalanches do happen, and even experts have been killed in them.

The mysteries of snow continue to fascinate and frustrate those working in the avalanche field. The mysteries of the human mind are no easier to unravel. When you combine snow and people in the avalanche zone, the outcome is hard to control.

Organizations like the Canadian Avalanche Centre do their best to provide backcountry travelers with a heads-up about potential dangers and hope that this work will save some lives. But the effects are impossible to accurately measure.

"It's a funny one," says Evan Manners of the CAC, "because sometimes when there's a storm, and no tragedy occurs,

83

it's hard to gauge whether it was the information that helped people avoid incidents, or was it just chance, or what was it? How do you count the avoided tragedies?"

{8}

YELLOW LIGHT

*

Sunday, December 28

"**H**ELLO, SILVER SPRAY CABIN. It's Dave calling from Slocan Chief. Over."

The voice seemed to jump out of the radio as Rob Driscoll and his friends were digging into their breakfast of cooked whole-grain cereal. Outside the window, the mountains had disappeared. Everything was socked in, and it had started to snow. A good morning for another cup of coffee. Lise Nicola leaped to her feet and headed to the radio.

"Hi, Dave. Lise here. Over."

Nicola knew Dave Heagy from her summers of working in the park. The personable Slocan Chief custodian was one of the rangers who'd interviewed her for the job. During the winter, Heagy was a partner in the company contracted by the parks branch to manage the two cabins in Kokanee Glacier Park. He and colleague Kevin Giles took turns staying in the little A-frame hut near the Slocan Chief cabin, one week on and one week off, and they hired custodians such as Nicola and Sean McTague for Silver Spray.

Each morning and evening, the custodians at the two cabins would check in with each other and with the parks district office down on the lakeshore highway, using a designated VHF radio frequency and repeater. Office staff would pass along the latest weather forecasts as well as the CAC avalanche bulletins that were issued twice a week, and the custodians relayed this information to their groups. In return, those on the mountain shared snow observations and information about the skiing they had been doing. Nicola had been up early that morning taking weather readings and recording them in the cabin log: obscured skies, 4 centimeters of snow in the past twenty-four hours, a high of −8°C and a low of −11.

"Okay, have a good day. I'll check in with you this evening," said Heagy, signing off at the end of their conversation.

"Yeah, talk to you later. Over and out," replied Nicola, and she returned to join the others.

After a pot or two of coffee, Lumpy Leidal was usually revved up, raring to hit the slopes and keeping the others smiling with his high-voltage enthusiasm. But when the group headed out to ski that morning, they were hampered by poor visibility. The ski terrain around the Silver Spray cabin tended to be high elevation and exposed. In good weather, the views were sublime, but during flat light, blizzards or whiteouts, there were few trees for visual reference. If a group's route-finding abilities with compass, altimeter and map were not first-rate, they could wander astray.

86   Hitch number two was the lack of avalanche-safe terrain easily accessed from the Silver Spray cabin. There were few slopes not steep enough to either produce avalanches or be threatened by avalanches from above. The miners who'd built the original shack hadn't been thinking about carving turns when they chose its location.

Still, the group got in some skiing that day. When Heagy checked in with Nicola by radio around six o'clock that evening, she asked if she could call him back, because she wanted to first discuss the day's snow observations with her group. Heagy noted that fact in his journal. The Silver Spray group seemed to be well aware of possible snow instability and actively monitoring it.

That evening, fat snowflakes fell outside the Silver Spray cabin. Inside, Leidal had the music cranked to the max. The others teased him about being in the mountains with a ghetto blaster, listening to obnoxious music. Fitzsimons and Driscoll cooked dinner, a garlic-free vegetarian meal that accommodated Nicola's food preferences. With a long evening stretching before them, there was plenty of time for people to relax and swap stories, recounting highlights of previous trips and past adventures.

Some of Von Blumen's and Leidal's wilder escapades had taken place during their teenage years in the early 1980s, when they'd been the youngest members of a group of hardcore mountain bikers hanging out at the Cove Bike Shop, in the Deep Cove area of North Vancouver. The shop and its owners, Chaz Romalis and Doug LaFavor, would go on to achieve legendary status in mountain biking circles. But at the time, most people thought the sport was some wacky fad from California that would never last. The riders who congregated there retrofitted old one-speed bikes, added gears, and then tested the results on the radically steep and rugged trails of Vancouver's North Shore mountains. Later the store brought in specialty mountain bikes from California, and when eighteen-year-old Von Blumen spent $1,200 on one, his father almost had a heart attack. Besides biking together, the Deep Cove fraternity skied, hung out, partied, camped under

87

the stars, traveled, looked out for each other and forged lasting friendships. "They lived the life," Leidal's mother, Carleen, would later say. "Those guys in their old age will have quite the memories of their youth. They were just a crazy bunch. They were hilarious, though it was frustrating for parents because none of them wanted to get an education or anything. But they were really nice, super guys."

One story about Leidal during that period dated from a group bike trip to Palm Springs. The guys were heading out for what they had assured their friend Greg Stone would be an easy ride. Stone had torn his shoulder apart the previous week when he'd jumped a washout in the road. His buddies had laughed like crazy when he'd crashed, of course, until they realized that he was too hurt to continue and would have to be dragged out of there. But after a week of lying by the pool, Stone figured he was good to go again, so he set off with the group. The "easy ride" turned out to be 80 kilometers of off-road torture. When Stone's shoulder had had enough, Leidal said no problem; he'd ride back for the group's truck and meet them at a road crossing ahead. But instead of returning with the truck, he arrived back on his bike with a six-pack of beer. He'd found a store in the middle of nowhere, and, figuring Stone needed something for his pain, he'd delivered the beer first. That done, he pedaled off again. No problem.

Scott Bradley hadn't been part of the Cove riding scene in those days; instead, he'd been a keen junior golfer. But he'd turned up at the Cove shop one day in the early '90s on a beater bike. After thrashing down the mountain on it, valiantly trying to keep pace with the others, he returned to the store a few days later to spend five grand on a new two-wheeler. From then on, he was nuts about the sport. One of

Bradley's former employees, Scott Belsey, remembers his boss gleefully recounting his mountain biking exploits at company staff meetings. Bradley would leap onto the seat of a chair, Belsey recalls, to reenact one of his spectacular falls off his bike.

Rob Driscoll's trove of stories included a three-day climbing epic as he and three friends scaled a huge pillar of rock called Wahoo Tower, which rises out of the ice of British Columbia's Coast Mountains. The bush pilot who flew them to the glacier landed abruptly in the middle of a crevasse field, breaking a tail ski. When he lifted off again, the ski was attached by a spare piece of rope. The pilot assured the group that he would not be returning to pick them up as planned, and he didn't. Oh, well. The four men climbed four pitches up the tower that afternoon, bivouacked on an uncomfortable ledge, and completed the final ten pitches to the top the following day. After a steep descent on snow, they walked 25 kilometers out to a road, crossing several dangerous creeks along the way. They functioned amazingly well considering that Driscoll, who was in charge of meals, had brought only minimal supplies: two packages of Kraft dinner per day for the entire group. Their final challenge was to locate at midnight a friend who was willing to drive into a remote logging camp to pick them up and take them home. The climbers let Driscoll make that phone call; he had the sort of friends who would rise to the occasion.

Outside Silver Spray, the falling snow was thickening. Inside, the wine flowed, the meal was delicious and Lumpy's music was raucous. Scott Bradley was in fine comic form, generating a lot of hilarity. Nicola's laugh, which friends claimed was twice as big as she was, filled the room.

MONDAY, DECEMBER 29

The next morning, Nicola reported 18 centimeters of new snow. With the storm came warmer temperatures and freezing levels up to 2000 meters. So although it was snowing rather than raining at Silver Spray, the flakes were wet and heavy, not the fluffy powder skiers prefer. The groups at both Silver Spray and the Slocan Chief had been warned on arrival about the underlying facet layers, and now they dug snowpits to take a look. "It was persistent on all aspects, this faceted snow," Cal Lloyd, one of the Utah skiers, would later recall. But they didn't have to dig at all to see evidence of the underlying instabilities. When the Silver Spray skiers climbed up the slope above their cabin, they saw so much cracking they turned tail and skied back down, one at a time.

That evening during the radio check, Nicola received the updated avalanche bulletin. It noted the recent storm snow and warming temperatures, and said that snow stability was generally poor. But things might be looking up.

"With any luck the warm storm conditions will have enough energy to reduce the widespread alien characteristics that exist in this untypical Columbia snowpack," the report stated. "Areas that were thin before the storm will be suspect because they have a heavily faceted base." But the hope was that once the new snow settled, it would help consolidate the snowpack. Even so, caution was advised. "This storm may leave us with a more easily managed snowpack for the New Year, but expect that specific areas will have deep weaknesses in the snowpack."

As the public bulletin indicated, there was a lot of uncertainty in the avalanche forecast. Some avalanche educators call these "yellow light" conditions. Using a traffic light system, they teach students how to decide when it's safe to ski certain slopes. A checklist guides participants through questions about terrain, snowpack and weather conditions, and they end up with an overall green, red or yellow light for skiing: Green—No hazard; Red—Danger, hazardous situation exists; Yellow—Caution, potential hazard exists, conditions are deteriorating or are uncertain. A red light should flash in skiers' minds any time steep, open slopes are combined with a hazardous snowpack. But the light changes to green if that hazardous snowpack rests on terrain not likely to avalanche— slopes of less than 30 degrees (some say 25 degrees), for example, or in dense trees that anchor the snow.

The decisions are thorniest during yellow-light conditions, which is why most fatal avalanches happen then. In a yellow-light situation, the avalanche hazard is probably rated "Considerable," and slope stability tests give results that are variable or in the middle range. You may get away with skiing on steep terrain at these times. Then again, you may not. Slopes that look benign can spring unwelcome surprises. With the snow balanced between stress and strength, one ski line might feel safe, while several meters to the side, where the terrain features are somewhat different, the snow will need only the weight of a skier to collapse.

"This is the time you really have to watch it," Dave Heagy always told the groups staying at the Slocan Chief cabin. He encouraged skiers to make conservative decisions and to leave a wide margin for error. As the December 29 avalanche bulletin suggested, conditions could improve; the weather could potentially help consolidate and stabilize the snowpack.

Or it could make things worse.

{9}

TOTALLY AWESOME

Tuesday, December 30

THE SAME MORNING that Rob Driscoll's group had flown
by helicopter to Silver Spray, a party of ten young male
professionals from Vancouver bumped, lurched and rattled in
a snow cat along the unplowed logging roads contouring up
the mountainside to the Ruby Creek cabin. The commercial
backcountry skiing lodge was about 50 kilometers northwest
of Silver Spray, and 500 meters lower, outside of the park in
the peaks of the Ruby Range. From there, the group would
head out each day to ski-tour the gladed slopes and alpine terrain above the cabin. With them was a professional guide
named Andrej Arajs.

The Ruby Creek party hadn't wanted to hire a guide.
Even at commercial lodges, many backcountry skiers don't
like to be told where to go or which terrain to ski, preferring
to rely on their own route-finding skills. Ruby Creek cabin
owner Dale Caton understood this and normally didn't insist
on a guide. But a scare the previous week had made him more
than usually anxious about the safety of his clients.

It had happened just prior to Christmas, before the cabin was open for the season, and at the same time that Marc Deschenes and his group were skiing at the Slocan Chief. Caton was taking some visiting relatives out for a short ski. From the Ruby Creek cabin they toured up gentle slopes through trees until they reached more open terrain. Before leading them up one particular alpine slope, Caton first dug a precautionary snowpit to take a quick look at the layers. He dug at his usual spot, about 2215 meters in elevation, because the slope angle and aspect there were similar to the terrain higher up.

Caton saw nothing in the pit or elsewhere that set off alarm bells, so the skiers toured partway up the slope and then took a short run down. Everyone was keen to go up again for a second run, and this time they ascended higher, all the way to the ridge.

But as Caton reached the top, there was a thunderous "whumph!" unlike anything he had heard in all his years in the mountains. It seemed to shoot out in all directions, reverberating around the basin. The noise astonished him; it was like an earthquake, maybe a freight train. It was so loud that Caton looked up at the sky to see if a jet was passing overhead.

A massive fracture must have occurred under the snow, Caton figured, although it didn't appear to have triggered any avalanches. He grabbed his shovel from his pack and dug down beneath his feet. What he saw within the snowpack at this elevation was quite different from what he'd seen at the base of the slope. Here, the bottom 60 centimeters of the snowpack had no strength or cohesion. Instead of a well-packed base, Caton found a crumbly foundation of unconsolidated, faceted crystals. The "whumph" he and his party had heard was the sound of air escaping as the unsupported upper snowpack dropped into that loose layer, like a collapsing

93

house of cards. Caton suggested that the skiers retreat to the forested slopes below.

After that ominous incident, Caton started to worry about the clients scheduled to arrive at the Ruby Creek cabin the following week. Their demographics put them squarely in the bull's eye of the group statistically most likely to be caught in an avalanche—young, aggressive males in their twenties. For their safety, as well as his own peace of mind, Caton prevailed on them to hire a guide for their visit. He gave them a good deal. Although reluctant, they finally agreed to use a guide for the first three days of their week-long stay.

That's why Andrej Arajs was with the Ruby Creek party as they broke trail through the latest snow just before noon on December 30. The storm that in the past three days had deposited 30 centimeters of new snow at Silver Spray had dumped a similar amount here. It was still snowing lightly, and the temperature was just a degree or two below freezing. Time to be extra vigilant, since most avalanches occur during or immediately after a snowstorm. With the warmer temperatures, this snow carried a hefty water content, making it even heavier.

Arajs stopped partway up the 28-degree slope, at 2200 meters elevation, and took out his shovel to dig a pit. He exposed a cross-section of the snowpack from surface to ground, smoothed the exposed vertical wall, and then poked and probed to identify the layers and check their density.

94 He already knew, more or less, what he was likely to find. Guides such as Arajs make it their business to take note of every weather event that can affect a snowpack over the course of the season. Digging snowpits allows them to monitor the progress of snow settlement, the effect of new snow loading,

the strengthening or weakening of previously noted layers, and the changes in both the shape of snow grains and how well they stick together. Guides may insert thermometers to measure the temperature gradient, or scrape off crystals for viewing under a magnifying loup. Some even eat the stuff, identifying crystal types by how they feel in the mouth. A guide's logbook is full of hieroglyphic-like notations describing crystal types and diameters, temperature gradients, snow density, water content, and current wind and weather.

Examining the 160-centimeter-deep snow face, Arajs measured about 36 centimeters of new snow atop older, partially settled snowfall. Deeper in the snowpack he found various instabilities, including a layer of surface hoar overlain by a hard crust. But it was one thing to identify these potentially weak layers and icy surfaces. The question was: how likely was it that the snow would slide?

One frequently used slope stability test is the rutschblock (a German word meaning "glide block"), a Swiss invention. That is the test Arajs proceeded to do. Having already exposed a two-meter-long wall of snow—about the length of a ski—he isolated a rectangular block of snow above this wall. First, he shoveled out the snow at either end for 1.5 meters (a ski-pole length) up the slope. Then he used a length of knotted cord to saw back and forth down the back wall of this test block, enlisting help from another skier to hold one end of the cord.

The rutschblock test involves having a volunteer on skis step sideways onto the isolated block of snow from the slope above. Once both skis are on the block, the skier lightly flexes his knees to give the snow a small jolt. If the block remains intact, he makes progressively more forceful jumps to see what it takes to fracture the snowpack within the block and set the top slab of snow sliding along the fracture plane.

The rutschblock scoring system ranges from one to seven. A one is given to a block that slides even as it is being cut out of the slope, before any additional weight is applied. A seven means that the block needs a lot of force to make it slide, if it ever slides at all. Low rutschblock scores indicate that slopes with similar conditions are likely to be triggered by a skier.

Arajs's results showed that the snowpack sheared moderately easily (a three) at the interface between the recent storm snow and previous deposits, with a harder shear (a five) at the surface hoar layer farther down. Although a rating of five would suggest that the surface hoar layer was not a huge concern at present at this site, Arajs knew that an avalanche could initiate on an easily sheared layer near the top of the snowpack and, once it got smoking, "step down" to a deeper layer, sending a much greater mass of snow crashing down the slope.

This foray into the snowpack provided some indication of the slope's stability, but Arajs would never decide to ski the run based on that information alone: he needed to put his snowpit findings into a broader context. He had chosen to bring his group into this area for several reasons. Less than 5 per cent of dry slab avalanches start on slopes under 30 degrees, so this moderate, 28-degree slope was less likely to slide. Also, he knew the area had been skied at the time of the surface hoar formation, as well as just a few days before. A well-tracked slope is more stable than one that hasn't been skied, because the smooth underlying layers (potential sliding surfaces) have been chopped up. Heli-ski companies will purposely track up certain slopes and keep them in their back pockets, in reserve, for times of high hazard. A subsequent snowfall will erase all traces of previous traffic, transforming a heavily used slope into a pristine, untracked ski run—but one that's now safer.

In addition, Arajs knew this slope wasn't one that normally slid under these conditions. That's the advantage local guides have over visitors who parachute into an area for a day or a week. Guides ski the same slopes season after season, developing an intimate knowledge of the terrain. They collect data on the snowpack all winter, noting features such as sun crusts (spots where the snow's surface has melted and subsequently frozen) and surface hoar layers before they become buried. Knowing where trigger zones and isolated weaknesses are can make the difference between traveling through an area unscathed and starting a big avalanche.

After filling in the rutschblock pit, the Ruby Creek group continued switchbacking up the hill, spacing out at the top to traverse the upper slope. Traveling well spaced is a precaution used when the avalanche risk is high; if a slide does run, it is less likely to take out the whole group. The skiers took a first run down through the powder, swooping in and out of glades to the flats below. Then they put their skins on to go back up for another run.

At the top, the first skier followed the tracks out across the upper slope. The tracks traversed a slight roll—a convex bulge in the slope. As Arajs followed about 20 meters behind, he heard and felt the snow settle beneath his feet. At the same moment, he saw a crack shoot across the slope, roughly along the line of the ski tracks, like a zipper opening. His added weight had triggered a shear in a weak layer underneath, and now that the overlying slab was unsupported it was starting to slip, with Arajs aboard. Cracks opened along each flank, and the slab started moving. It slid as if on ball bearings, picked up speed, broke into chunks and took its passenger for

97

a heart-pounding ride down the hill. Arajs was deposited at the bottom uninjured and still upright on his skis, but standing on a pile of avalanche debris up to two meters deep.

Arajs later estimated the size of the avalanche as Class 2. The slide path was 75 meters wide. The slab, 80 to 100 centimeters thick, had slid on the surface hoar layer.

The avalanche was breathtaking, but what happened next was, as Arajs noted in his otherwise technical report to the Canadian Avalanche Centre, "totally awesome." The shock waves from the first slide set off a spectacular chain reaction, with fracture lines shooting out across neighboring slopes. On slope after slope, long cracks ripped open the snow just below the ridge tops, letting loose massive slides. In seconds, the skiers were engulfed in a swirling powder cloud, a sudden blizzard of white that blotted out the entire basin. Arajs later estimated the size of this second slide, which released on adjacent slopes, as Class 3.

All in all, it was a spectacular and sobering display of the phenomenon of sympathetic avalanche releases, and it illustrated just how far an initial avalanche can propagate when conditions are right. The snow had formed a dense slab, which must have been under great tension in some spots. Cutting across the slab with skis at a vulnerable point was like slicing a knife through tightly stretched fabric—once the crack started, it shot out lickety-split across one slope, and the next, setting off slides like dominoes falling in sequence. Someone standing on what seemed like a safe slope a kilometer away could easily have been taken for a ride.

THAT EVENING, when Evan Manners received a fax at the Canadian Avalanche Centre with an initial report on this incident from Dale Caton, it was the evidence he had been waiting for. Manners had a gut feeling that a particularly dangerous situation was developing in the south Columbia Mountains. The snowpack might eventually consolidate and improve, but in the meantime he was concerned that the recent snow had put yet more stress on precarious slopes. Despite his uneasiness, there had been no major red flags—until now. Manners knew Andrej Arajs; the two of them had worked together as ski bums at Lake Louise back in the early 1980s. If an experienced guide such as Arajs could be surprised by a slide, it indicated a scary snowpack. And as Arajs's report illustrated, the snow had a great potential for propagating. This would be important information to incorporate into the public bulletin Manners would start writing tomorrow.

Over at the Silver Spray cabin, Lise Nicola listened to Dave Heagy pass on the results of the slope stability tests done at the Slocan Chief that day—more variable scores, shearing mostly in the upper snowpack under the new storm snow. Heagy also told Nicola about an avalanche on a southwest-facing slope that the Utah group had triggered. It was on a steep section of a known avalanche slope that he had specifically recommended the skiers avoid. Near the top of the slope, a shallow layer of snow covered a rock band. Places like that are notorious trigger zones; the warmer rock promotes crystal growth, which results in poor bonding. Although several members of the group had cautiously avoided the rock outcropping, others had skied down over it. As the third skier descended, the snow beneath his feet began to move. It slid right from the ground, where the rock face was covered with ice. The accelerating snow pulled the skier down towards some trees; he managed to twist around so he hit them skis first. But the sliding snow was still coming down, threatening to bury him. He turned his skis downhill and went with the slide. His guardian angel must have been on duty that day, because although the skiers later estimated a Class 2 avalanche with a width of 75 meters, he wound up at the bottom of the slope buried only to his knees. Just a scare, this time.

Another person who was carefully monitoring the deteriorating conditions in the snowpack was Dave Smith, the Nelson region's avalanche control technician. The snow on some of Smith's active avalanche paths was becoming increasing unstable, and it would eventually threaten major roads in the region. How much more load could those slopes handle? It was crucial that he catch them at the right moment. He didn't want to bomb before the snow was ready to move, yet he needed to do it before the slopes avalanched naturally onto unsuspecting drivers below. Smith would be keeping close tabs on his test sites to see what happened. What would the outcome of the next storm be? For everybody concerned about slides in the region, the watch was on.

{10}

BRINGING IN THE NEW YEAR

*

Wednesday, December 31

LISE NICOLA was doing Tai Chi on the packed-down heli pad, the mountain view stretching out before her as she moved through her form. Her friend Monica Nissen had reacted in mock horror when Nicola had admitted that, lately, she liked Tai Chi even more than skiing. But over the past year Nicola had been exploring new aspects of herself, widening her previously all-consuming focus on outdoor pursuits.

Her Tai Chi set complete, she stood quietly looking out at the landscape, slowing her breathing. Earlier she had recorded the weather readings in the log, and for the first time since they arrived she hadn't had to draw the circle with an X through it that indicated "obscured" sky conditions. Instead, this morning she had drawn circles slashed by one and two vertical lines, to represent scattered and broken clouds. Knowing that this better weather wasn't supposed to last, she took in the view while she could.

Nicola loved being in the mountains, and her passion for the outdoors had always been the driving force in her life. The interest sparked by family trips as a child had been reinforced when she took part in major backpacks and ski trips in the Rockies as part of her Calgary high school's outdoors program. Since that time she had been impossible to keep up with, always on adventures with like-minded friends on her days off, climbing or skiing or kayaking. She would arrive home from holidays the night before she was due back at work, and not a moment sooner.

Her climb the previous May up 5959-meter Mount Logan had been the culmination of her adventures so far. There had been six of them on the twenty-two-day climb, all from the Kootenay area. The dehydrated curries and other meals concocted during months of preparation had turned out to be so delicious that the climbers had dubbed their trip the Kootenay Potluck Tour. She and Wren McElroy had been the only women, not that gender was a big factor on the trip. They both had the physical strength, determination and drive to make sure that they were as capable as the men.

The day they had planned to summit was stormy, and although two of the men had pushed to the top, the others had turned back. Nicola had been in tears, but the next morning the weather miraculously cleared and the final four climbers were on their way by 7:30 AM. They abandoned their skis when the snow got icy and hard, continuing with crampons on their boots. The last pitch was too steep even to rope up; one person falling would have pulled the others down 4000 meters. It was the most exposed walk Nicola had ever taken. With each step she'd kicked the front points of her crampons into the slope, dug in her ice ax and rested before pulling herself up for another step. Trip organizer Keyes Lessard was in the lead, Derek Marcoux next, then Nicola, with Wren McElroy right behind her. Finally, they'd reached the summit. It was cold and windy with a clear 360-degree view, and nothing, anywhere in Canada, was higher.

The next day the group had descended 3000 meters to their base camp. The following morning, after the small plane had landed on the glacier twice to scoop up the four men, she and Wren sat waiting for their turn to leave. They were flooded with a sense of achievement and appreciation. After being on the mountain for three weeks, hot showers and fresh food sounded inviting, yet they were loath to leave such a special place. The trip had been phenomenal, and they knew it would be a touchstone they would think about in future years.

Nicola and her fellow Logan expedition members had decided to put together a slide show about the climb, which was scheduled for presentation in Nelson on February 1. She would finish preparing her part of it when she got home.

Today, after a last look at the Selkirk Mountains to the south, Nicola turned and walked down the path to the cabin for breakfast.

Taking advantage of the improved weather, all of the group except Carrie Fitzsimons toured uphill from the cabin that morning, to the col between McQuarrie and Sunrise mountains. The men took turns breaking trail, setting a contoured track the others could follow. Lumpy Leidal tended to charge upslope, his big lungs custom-designed for climbing hills. Nicola liked to stay at the back of the line, where she could help any stragglers. On a well-laid uphill track, the skiers could get into a rhythm that was almost meditative, sliding forward onto one ski and then the other, planting one pole and then the other, trudging up and up in single file.

It was the last day of 1997. For Nicola, it had been a particularly good year. After some difficult periods recently when she had bounced from one job to another, struggling to find her path, things had coalesced. She was happy with her decision to become a teacher. Mount Logan had been an amazing experience that boosted her confidence. The year had included other highlights, too, such as a September biking trip with her father and younger brother along the abandoned Kettle Valley railroad that snaked over high trestles and through tunnels. And here she was, ending the year high in the mountains. As she climbed, she felt their powerful presence around her. She heard the snow crunching under her skis, the slight clinking as one ski edge scraped the other, and the huff and puff of her breath.

When the skiers reached their high point, the col between Sunrise and McQuarrie, close by the spot where miners a century earlier had dug shafts in search of silver, they stopped to munch on gorp and glug plastic-scented drink from their water bottles. A new view lay before them, although the distant peaks were shrouded in clouds. On a good day, Nicola knew, you could even see the black towers of the Bugaboos, a prime rock climbing area 100 kilometers away in the Purcell Range. She and her friend Alice Weber had spent five glorious days there the previous August. They had driven to the trailhead in Nicola's old truck, Tom Petty and Indigo Girls in the tape deck, talking about pretty much everything. With Nicola's encouragement, Weber had pushed herself to lead their routes up Pigeon Spire and Donkey's Ears, then belayed Nicola so she could also tackle the legendary black pinnacles. The trip had been exhilarating for both of them.

Nicola stripped off her climbing skins, folded them into her pack and prepared for some downhill turns with the group. They were standing at the portal over the height of land and onto the Caribou Glacier on the north side of the skiing area. From here they would pick a downhill run, so they checked the map and discussed the direction in which they should proceed. Sometimes the skiing on these north-facing slopes of the glacier was fantastic. Under ideal conditions, the snow beneath your skis felt smooth as satin, soft as goose down. You'd float on air, carve turns through whipped cream, sail over bumps and land in bottomless clouds of powder. It was the closest thing to flying. But not today. The group was disappointed to find that the wind had packed the recent snow and formed a hard crust. This was definitely not the champagne powder they had dreamed about.

A few hours later, as the skiers returned to the col and then headed back to the cabin, the clouds were thickening again, and the party found themselves negotiating the slope in flat light. It looked as if there would be more snow before the new year arrived.

DOWN AT THE Canadian Avalanche Centre office in Revelstoke, Evan Manners was preparing the public bulletin that would be issued the next day, January 1, 1998. He had access to the previous day's reports from the industry exchange, and he'd talked to Andrej Arajs about his experience in the slide at Ruby Creek. Manners was also in possession of an ominous weather forecast. A huge trough of dense, cold air from the Arctic was moving south, seeping through the mountain passes into British Columbia's interior. Temperatures were predicted to plunge. Although the weather systems in winter blew inland from the Pacific, the maritime storms occasionally collided with arctic air masses flowing into the province from the northeast. Common on the prairies, those arctic flows didn't always manage to penetrate British Columbia's mountain defenses. Even when they did, they could be deflected east again during a shoving match with the prevailing winds from the coast. But sometimes, when the westerly Pacific flow had already lost strength, the dense, ground-hugging arctic flows brought prolonged periods of clear weather and low temperatures. When the lighter Pacific air mass flowed over the colder air, the result could be a whopping dump of snow until the arctic air mass was pushed out.

This was the scenario that was forecast on December 31, and it wasn't encouraging—on the contrary. The rate at which snow falls has a direct bearing on the avalanche hazard. A slope loaded lightly and slowly can gradually adjust and settle. But snow doesn't like rapid changes, and a sudden weighting can cause the snowpack to crack. Avalanche educators usually bring some Silly Putty along to their classes, to demonstrate how a substance can be slowly stretched but will crack and fracture if pulled apart suddenly. As Manners saw it, emerging conditions were a formula for avalanches, and the bulletin he prepared for release on January 1 reflected that.

South Columbia Mountains

Weather: The south country has seen new snow and warm temperatures to end 1997. An arctic airmass is pouring over the divide from Alberta January 1st, and will cause a sharp drop in temperatures. A Pacific low is heading inland, and will be forced over the dome of cold air, making for a big dump of snow to start off 1998. The Pacific air will be inland by late Friday, and skies will be clear and temperatures around −20. The arctic air will begin to slowly mix, and temperatures will be a little warmer each day. Pronounced instability will produce swirling winds at the airmass interface, while areas in Pacific air will have moderate west winds and areas in the arctic air will be relatively calm.

Snowpack: The avalanche cycle from the storm snow last week is still going on, and more snow will fall on that. Instabilities are most pronounced in the upper 40 cm, but many avalanches are stepping down into lower problem layers. Crusts, facets, weak layers bridged by thin strong layers, buried surface hoar, the south Columbias has it all right now. The most dangerous layer is the December surface hoar down about 75–100 cm, which in one case produced an avalanche 1 km wide in the New Denver area.

Avalanches: Widespread natural and skier-triggered activity still being reported to January 1, before the heavy snow begins. Activity will increase as this new snow is added rapidly, then taper off later in the weekend.

Danger: High, improving through the weekend to Considerable by Sunday.

Travel Advisory: Watch out, here comes a big one! Although things will tighten up and natural activity taper off by Saturday, use caution before you rip into the dump with that new sled or board you got for Christmas.

In Kokanee Glacier Park, the anticipated "big dump of snow" began on New Year's Eve. Earlier that day, Dave Heagy had noted in his diary that two natural avalanches had run down south-facing slopes across the valley from the Slocan Chief cabin—an example of the "natural activity" reported in the bulletin.

Driscoll's group at Silver Spray had a hoot that evening, celebrating in a snow cave they dug out of the slope. There were no neighbors to complain when the party became raucous.

THURSDAY, JANUARY 1, 1998

New Year's Day, waking to a whiteout, the groups at both Silver Spray and the Slocan Chief skied in a blizzard. The snow was deep and wet, soaking their clothing in no time. "It was just dumping," remembers Cal Lloyd of the Utah group. "It was so heavy you really had to find a steeper slope, somewhere you could get your momentum going, because it was pushing up against your thighs." Even when Lloyd's party skied straight down the fall line, they never got going very fast. It was like waterskiing behind a slow boat.

The group at Silver Spray stayed in the trees along the lower edge of Clover Basin, but it was heavy going there, too. After they were tired of skiing porridge, they returned to the cabin to shovel paths, haul water and carry armloads of firewood from the woodshed. Fitzsimons was cooking dinner. With wet clothes steaming on wall hooks, faces scoured by the wind, hair matted, muscles spent, sweaty socks peeled off and toes wriggling gratefully ... after a day like the one they'd had, it was absolute heaven for the group to sit back with wine or cups of tea, gazing out the window at the darkening landscape. The glow from the cabin's propane lights reflected off the fat snowflakes still whirling around the cabin.

That evening, when the CAC's avalanche bulletin was relayed to the hut custodians, Lise Nicola sat by the radio listening and taking notes. She transferred the pertinent information into the weather log in the cabin. "Avalanche cycle ongoing. Naturals widespread," she wrote, noting the lower snowpack instability on the December 8 surface hoar layer. The rest of her group overheard the transmission, and the storm that would deposit a further load on the slopes during the night had already begun.

While the inhabitants of the Silver Spray hut snuggled into their sleeping bags, winds swooped in from the north, picking up the unsettled snow and sweeping it over ridges onto the lee slopes, including those of nearby Clover Basin. Each time the velocity of the wind doubles, the amount of snow it can carry increases by a factor of eight. The delicate snow crystals were transformed by tumbling and colliding with each other into small, rounded grains that packed into soft slabs.

By the time the eastern sky began to brighten outside the windows of Silver Spray, tonnes of snow—billions of individual crystals held together by icy bonds and static friction—hung from the slopes encircling Clover Basin. Without X-raying the snowpack, it would be impossible to tell where in the variable terrain the snow would have the strength and stability to support the extra weight of a skier, and where that stress would be unbearable. The snow was engaged in a silent tug-of-war with the forces of gravity. All it needed to let loose was a trigger in the right spot. In theory, even one snowflake could tip the scale.

THE MOUNTAIN SHRUGGED

Friday, January 2

OVERNIGHT, the storm moved on. The skiers in Kokanee Glacier Park woke on Friday to a gloriously cold, sparkly morning. "It was a bluebird day," recalls Cal Lloyd. The two groups were almost giddy at the gift of sun shimmering on drifts of fresh powder after a week of cloudy skies and crummy visibility. Dave Heagy measured 39 centimeters of snow in the past twenty-four hours at the Slocan Chief cabin. At Silver Spray, Nicola recorded 31 centimeters of new snow. Temperatures were dropping. The winds were blowing strongly from the northwest. During Heagy and Nicola's radio check that morning, they talked about the storm and the previous day's avalanche bulletin.

The evening before, the Silver Spray group had discussed a plan for their last day in the mountains. Soon they would be back to the strains and stresses of regular life. And the luxuries, too; a bath would definitely be a good idea. But before that, the best weather and snow conditions of the entire week lay waiting for them. They'd decided they would traverse over to the forested slopes below Woodbury Mountain, an area known as the Woodbury glades. The ski runs there would be relatively safe because the slopes were less steep and the trees would help to anchor the snow. To get to those slopes, however, they would have to travel to the far side of Clover Basin, the wide, open bowl below Sunrise Mountain.

In summer, Clover Basin is a sloping, hummocky, boulder-strewn meadow rich with wildflowers and huckleberries and drained by tumbling Silver Spray Creek. Hikers slogging up the steep trail from the Woodbury valley, heading for the Silver Spray cabin, emerge from the forest and traverse this subalpine basin, stopping to bask in the south-facing exposure or take in the superb views.

In winter, the bowl can be a fantastic thigh-burner of a ski run as far down as a skier is willing to climb up again. The vertical drop is several hundred meters. But Clover Basin contains some known avalanche paths, so the snowpack has to be stable to ski those lines. Today, the group wouldn't spend much time in the basin but would traverse it instead.

Carrie Fitzsimons decided she was not up to an energetic day of skiing and elected to stay in the cabin. Lise Nicola was also planning to stay behind, to deal with custodial chores such as cleaning the cabin, shoveling the pathway to the outhouse and stomping down the helipad with snowshoes. However, when some of the guys offered to help her with this work afterwards if she wanted to join them on the slopes, she rushed to get ready.

The skiers stuffed their lunches into their backpacks along with the usual gear for a day of skiing in the mountains. Then Driscoll, Leidal, Von Blumen, Cowan, Bradley and Nicola headed out the door to put on their skis.

What a morning! The sun was shining, and those rays felt so good. Time to dig out the sunglasses. Once set to go, the group skied towards the rim of the basin, their tracks slicing through the blanket of undisturbed whiteness. The cooler temperatures had helped to dry out the snow, and the top layer was light and fluffy. On such a morning, when the sky is the color of forget-me-nots and the snow is soft as baby powder, it's hard to believe anything could ever go wrong. Less than a minute later, the skiers dropped over the edge and down the side of the bowl into Clover Basin.

Photographs later developed from Driscoll's camera indicate that he probably skied down first and took photos of the others making their turns. It was common for either Driscoll or Von Blumen to be first down the slope and for the other to come down last, after watching the rest of the party descend. In the event that skiers are caught by a slide, you want someone watching where the avalanche takes them, so they can be dug out quickly. The group seems to have skied down onto a flat bench within the basin.

Either before that or after, they dug a snowpit. Notes later discovered in Leidal's backpack, dated that morning, indicate that the skiers performed a standard shear test to gauge slope stability.

Back in the cabin, Carrie Fitzsimons did the dishes and read her novel.

AT THE SLOCAN CHIEF cabin, the group from Utah was having a primo day of skiing on the big, open northwest-facing slopes. The new snow was light, fluffy and fast, and they were able to float above the heavy mush they had been skiing the previous day.

Cal Lloyd could hear his companions "hootin' and hol-
lerin'" from up on the hill. In a case of very poor timing, he
himself was cabin-bound, suffering from flu symptoms. "Our
guys came in with big huge smiles," he remembers. "It was
the best day of their trip."

Many people enjoyed skiing in the mountains of the south
Columbias that day. They didn't all make headlines. A lot of
them, mindful of the new snow that would be loading slopes
with buried instabilities, and perhaps having read the avalanche bulletin, probably chose their travel routes conserva-
tively. Others probably didn't, but they were lucky.

Mount Carlyle is a 2673-meter peak about 10 kilometers
north of the Silver Spray cabin, just outside the boundaries of
Kokanee Glacier Park. On that same "bluebird" morning, a
party of backcountry skiers staying at a nearby commercial
cabin was breaking trail through the fresh snow within sight
of the mountain. At about 10:30 AM, they were treated to an
awesome display as they watched a large, naturally triggered
avalanche sweep down the slope of Mount Carlyle and across
a lake below. Wow! They knew the steep alpine slope was
prone to avalanches, but nothing like this. The whopper of a
slide ran with such force that it actually scooped the ice off the
lake, carrying huge chunks over the far bank and leaving
them scattered about 30 meters down the slope beyond.

That avalanche was only one of many in the southern
Selkirks that day. Most of the slides tumbled down in remote
or uninhabited areas where there were no observers. Some,
however, were far too close for comfort. At one cat-skiing
operation north of the park, the driver of a snow cat heading
up an access road had a close encounter when a wall of snow
swept over his machine. The avalanche broke the windshield

and trapped the driver inside, forcing him to exit through the roof vent.

LATER THAT MORNING, back at Silver Spray, Fitzsimons put on her boots and went outside with her binoculars to see if she could spot the others on the far side of Clover Basin. She walked up to the crest of the rocky rise outside the cabin, from which she could see across the bowl, although not down into it. "I couldn't see any tracks in the trees and wasn't sure if perhaps they hadn't got there," she would later recall. "I could see a small slide on the far side of the basin, but I couldn't see the full basin because of the aspect. Just some debris at the edge."

She went back inside and tried calling Nicola on the radio. When she didn't get an answer, she checked to see if Nicola had, in fact, taken a radio with her that day. One of the three seemed to be missing from the cabin, so she assumed their hut custodian had it with her. Fitzsimons called again. Still no answer. She went back outside. "Rob?" she shouted. "Pat?" She yelled a number of times.

Fitzsimons was an experienced physician, used to handling crises and dealing with emergencies; nurses at the hospital praised her calm and competent manner under pressure. She was not someone who was easily spooked or panicked. Just the same, she *was* concerned; the backcountry made her nervous. She had never been entirely comfortable there.

"Rob?" she shouted again.

Silence. The massive black-granite pillars of nearby Sunrise Mountain loomed over the white slopes of the basin. A sea of snow-covered peaks receded into the far distance.

Silence, and not another soul in sight.

SIXTEEN KILOMETERS west of the Silver Spray cabin, again just outside of the park boundaries, eight young men were ski-touring along a ridge beneath a peak known as Mount Aylwin. They had accessed the area by snowmobile from the Slocan Valley west of Kokanee Glacier Park and were staying at a nearby cabin, one of those unauthorized hideaways in the mountains that all of the locals claim to know nothing about.

A couple of the men were from out of town, but the rest were resident powder hounds who spent many days each winter exploring the nearby slopes. One of them had been in the mountains skiing virtually every day for the past month, part of a marathon effort to quit smoking. Several of the men had avalanche training and some were on their way to becoming ski guides, so the group was experienced and aware of the deep instabilities in the snowpack. They'd done some ski cuts that morning and tested a few slopes but couldn't get anything to release.

They hiked to one potential run off the ridge and dug a snowpit near the top, but they didn't like what it indicated about the stability of the slope. They backtracked to another spot; the snow profile there looked somewhat better, and the slope itself had different terrain features and more trees to anchor the snow. They figured it would be safe to ski.

About 1:30 PM, two members of the group, Kevin Jewitt and Simon Lewis, made the first wiggly tracks through the knee-deep powder while Lewis's dog, Sketch-dog, bounded after them. The men halted on a bench below to wait for the others. A third skier made a couple of turns before stopping on a slight rise in the middle of the slope. A fourth man dropped from the ridge onto the run, but as he executed his first turn, the whole slope gave way. It may have been the last skier who triggered the slide or, as one of the group suggested later, the dog's weight on the snow that caused the weak layer beneath to collapse, the underlying shear propagating like a wave up the slope to the starting zone. Whatever had caused it, a 30-meter-wide slab released, flowed down both sides of the rise where the third skier was still standing and tumbled 300 meters down onto the two men waiting below. There was no time to react. The avalanche swept them over the bench and down a further steep slope to the valley bottom.

It took more than twenty minutes for the remaining skiers to pinpoint the two radio sources beneath the huge mound of snow, dig down through the solidified debris and extricate their friends. By then, Kevin Jewitt and Simon Lewis were dead.

January days are short, and with darkness moving in, the rest of the group was forced to make their way down the mountain, leaving the bodies of their friends behind. It would be two days before the bodies could be retrieved.

Another slide on January 2 was responsible for the first avalanche death reported that day in British Columbia. Snowmobiler Murray Perrin, from Medicine Hat, Alberta, had been out sledding with friends in the Rocky Mountains near the town of Sparwood, almost at the Alberta border. When the mountain shrugged off its load of snow, the avalanche caught them by surprise, sweeping over four of their sleds. Perrin's companions survived the slide, but by the time they located him and dug him out, Perrin was dead.

BY EARLY AFTERNOON, fog was rolling towards the Silver Spray cabin, and Carrie Fitzsimons's anxiety was mounting. "You're just being paranoid," she told herself. "You've been that way all week."

Still, she wondered whether she should ski down into the basin to look for any sign of the group. "No, that would be crazy," she thought. "Absolutely crazy to go down there alone."

Many things could have happened to delay the party—a broken binding, a sprained ankle, route-finding problems. This was a group of competent outdoors people who could handle emergencies. Even if they didn't return before dark, they would probably spend the night huddled in a snow cave they'd dug, keeping each other warm with ribald jokes, and then find their way back in the morning.

So Fitzsimons waited, the novel abandoned (she never did finish it), until the early winter dusk showed signs of settling over the snowy landscape. Finally, at close to four o'clock, she tried to raise someone else on the radio.

Dave Heagy had enjoyed a dynamite day of skiing, one of the best, but he was now back in the little A-frame hut, a short walk from the Slocan Chief cabin. He picked up Fitzsimons's call, as did his partner Kevin Giles, who had the radio on in his kitchen down in Nelson. Fitzsimons explained that the Silver Spray party had not come back. They weren't answering the radio. She was getting worried.

The men suggested that Fitzsimons go outside again before it got too dark and take another careful look in the direction the group had gone. When she returned, she reported seeing tracks from the cabin heading for some avalanche debris that was visible at the edge of the basin. She tried to convince herself that the tracks were from the day before, realizing only later that since it had snowed overnight, the previous tracks would no longer be visible.

Whether the missing skiers were just delayed or something worse had occurred, nothing could be done for them in the dark. In his A-frame hut, Heagy switched to a somewhat more private frequency, bypassing the repeater, and continued to talk to Fitzsimons across the dark mountains.

AS SOON AS he got off the air in Nelson, Kevin Giles followed standard after-hours emergency procedures by alerting the local Royal Canadian Mounted Police. The RCMP dispatcher then phoned the RCMP in Kaslo, a village 70 kilometers north of Nelson along the twisting road bordering Kootenay Lake. An invisible line separated Kootenay Glacier Park into two different RCMP jurisdictions, and the Silver Spray area was the responsibility of the much smaller Kaslo detachment.

Corporal Doug McCowan and Constable Jay Arnold were patrolling the streets of Kaslo that Friday night, dropping by the hotel bar, keeping an eye out for people drinking on the street or traffic violations—the usual routine. The Kaslo detachment was technically a three-person operation, but it was short one officer in January 1998. With a population of less than a thousand, the village didn't usually require a large police contingent.

After receiving the call from the RCMP dispatcher about a missing party of skiers in Kokanee Glacier Park, McCowan and Arnold hustled back to the small detachment office. McCowan lived in one half of the low brick building, and the RCMP office took up the other side. Behind the front counter were three desks—one for the secretary who had already gone home, and two workstations. Beyond that were a small room containing a Breathalyzer and a jail cell.

The officers lost no time in hitting the phones, readying a search for the following morning. "It's usually at night that we get the call, and we will typically not send a crew up looking in the dark," says Arnold. "You can't fly, for one thing.

And where the area is, it's not accessible to walk up there."

Not that a two-man detachment had the resources to carry out a major search anyway. McCowan called Kaslo's volunteer search and rescue leaders to enlist their help. Although the RCMP would remain in overall command, they could call in resources as needed, and in this case they wanted the local search and rescue group to assist with the operational aspects of the search. The RCMP would provide administrative backup, contact families and respond to media inquiries.

British Columbia's network of volunteer search and rescue (SAR) crews runs under the umbrella of the Provincial Emergency Program. Kaslo's group is part of this network, as is a group based in Nelson. Trained volunteers can be called out for any emergency situation, but it is usually to conduct searches for lost or missing persons. On a big search, search and rescue teams in neighboring communities back each other up.

SAR civilians usually operate under what's called the Incident Command System. The RCMP officer in charge of the investigation, Corporal McCowan in this case, is at the top of the command hierarchy; immediately underneath is a search and rescue "Incident Commander," a role taken on by a volunteer who has undergone the requisite training. Other volunteers are assigned roles corresponding to boxes on the organizational chart—section chiefs, directors, team leaders and so on down the line. Search leaders can also bring in outsiders with particular expertise, such as specialists in avalanche rescue.

119

What unfolded in January 1998 was a little different from the usual scenario. The leaders of the Kaslo Search and Rescue group, Andy Tyers and Paddy Flanagan, were called to the RCMP office Friday evening for a briefing, and they subsequently set in motion their own procedures, beginning with obtaining a task number from the Provincial Emergency Program headquarters in Victoria to cover operational costs and medical insurance. Then they phoned their members to have them ready for the following morning. But a cluster of key people in Nelson were also involved in organizing the search right from the get-go. As soon as he had reported the missing party to the RCMP, Kevin Giles started making phone calls to the most experienced avalanche people he knew in town.

One of the first people Giles called was Dave Smith, arguably the most respected avalanche professional in Nelson. Besides his experience with highway avalanche control, Smith was a long-time mountain guide. Low-key and thoughtful, he was the kind of guy who knew his stuff, did his job and didn't make a big deal about it. But when he talked, people tended to listen.

Smith immediately asked who was in the missing party. When he learned that Lise Nicola was in the group, and that she had a radio but hadn't reported in, alarm bells went off. He was projecting way ahead, since he had no concrete evidence yet that the group had been caught in an avalanche. But he was well aware of the current instability in the snowpack. He had met Nicola the previous fall at a work party to replace the roof on the Slocan Chief cabin, and he knew of her experience in the outdoors. If Driscoll's group was benighted due to a problem such as a broken leg, Nicola should have been able to reach a ridge top to make radio contact and let everybody know what was happening.

After Smith put down the phone, he sat and thought about likely scenarios. If, when the searchers flew into the area the following morning, they discovered that Driscoll's party had been involved in an avalanche, the first step would likely be to make the slope safe for the rescue party. That could mean using explosives to bring down any snow that was still hanging from the slopes and might fall onto the track. Although just a volunteer at this point, Smith had access to equipment and facilities through his job that could be critical to the rescue. And the searchers would waste valuable time if he had to fly back out from the avalanche site to get organized before flying back in to do a bombing run.

After a few hours, Smith drove down to his work headquarters and collected what he would need to access his explosive magazine and do a bomb run the next day. Getting everything ready was just a precaution, because he hadn't yet given up hope. As he remembers, "I decided I would remain optimistic that the radio had quit, that it ran out of batteries, that they had somebody down with a broken ankle and they were all camped out overnight keeping that person warm and would get back in the morning. Things like that can happen."

Another veteran avalanche expert who received a call that night from Kevin Giles was Tom Van Alstine. As a park ranger and former snow safety supervisor at the local Whitewater ski hill, Van Alstine had coordinated many search and rescue operations in the backcountry beyond ski-area boundaries. He was also a paramedic and a first aid instructor. Tall and lanky, he projected an aura of quiet competence—an asset in any rescue scenario.

Giles also phoned Marc Deschenes, the heli-ski guide who had come down from the Slocan Chief cabin the previous week. "When I heard from Kevin that they weren't back, I thought, this can't be good," recalls Deschenes, although at the time he figured that they'd be dealing with a lost party or a broken leg. He agreed to be ready at first light to participate in the search.

Before packing his rescue kit, Deschenes made a call of his own to a colleague with whom he taught avalanche courses. John Buffery, known to his many friends as "Buf," was a slight, wiry man with a ruddy face and a balding pate encircled by wayward hair. He'd joked that he'd wanted to play a hobbit in the *Lord of the Rings* films, and friends thought he'd have been a natural for the part. Buffery was another import from urban Toronto who had tasted the mountains and rivers of British Columbia and never gone back. He had parlayed his extensive expertise as a ski and river-rafting guide into jobs all over the world, as an on-site safety consultant for IMAX films, extreme adventure races and Hollywood movie productions such as *Shanghai Knights* and *K2*. Those gigs, plus ski guiding jobs and contracts to teach avalanche courses, led to a somewhat crazy, itinerant lifestyle that Buffery didn't always manage to keep up with. But Nelson was home, and when Deschenes called, Buf agreed to be part of the initial response team the next day.

One other person was already lined up to assist: Terry Barter, the dog handler with the Nelson RCMP. Barter's dog was often called in to help find a party missing in the mountains, and Jay Arnold had contacted Barter first thing so that he could free up time to take part in the search. In addition to requesting the services of Barter's dog, the Kaslo detachment would use Barter as a source of advice about search logistics and as the RCMP's point-man in the field.

Barter had been working with avalanche dogs for twenty years, and his current sidekick was a big, Eastern European–bred German shepherd called Bela. Bela had a home in the back of Barter's pickup, which was kept parked outside the Nelson RCMP detachment. The truck was loaded with Barter's skis and boots as well as packs equipped for various scenarios. In his job, you never knew what the day would bring.

Barter had the close-clipped hair and forceful presence of a veteran police officer. After years of involvement in stressful, sometimes gruesome search and rescue scenarios, he had also developed a protective thick skin and a strong streak of black humor.

Barter had spent the afternoon of January 2 making preparations to head for the fatal avalanche that had buried the snowmobiler near Sparwood. When searchers found Murray Perrin's body, that mission was called off. Now there was a missing party up in Kokanee Glacier Park, but Barter wasn't overly concerned. He knew that the missing skiers were knowledgeable and experienced in the outdoors, and they would know enough to sit tight. "Ninety per cent of the time people are just overdue," Barter says. As for the lack of radio contact, radios are line-of-sight. "I travel in the backcountry with a radio all the time, and it's one of the first things you want to throw against a rock face. Besides weighing a pound, half the time it doesn't work."

It was arranged that Kevin Giles would fly up to the Silver Spray cabin first thing in the morning with hut custodian Sean McTague, who was supposed to be taking over from Nicola, anyway. Those two would take a quick look around. The next group of skiers booked for the cabin was ready to fly in, knowing nothing about the missing party. Everyone was still hoping for the best. With any luck, Driscoll's group would be found by Giles and McTague, cold but fine.

If necessary, however, a top-notch initial response team was set to go. There weren't many places where you could pack so much avalanche rescue expertise into a team at such short notice. The Nelson team consisted of experienced professionals who knew and trusted each other. And the Kaslo Search and Rescue group was ready to back them up. If they had to, they could later call for assistance from the Nelson SAR group. But it was best not to have too many people involved during the early stages of a search, putting themselves at risk, until it was clear what the situation required.

"It was really good," recalls Buffery. "No pressure, no hype, just a real clear initial response team with a wealth of experience. That was all we needed for right then and there. Then, as it developed, we could bring in other resources." Terry Barter concurs. "If there was anything that stands out in this one, it was the abundance of real expertise that we had."

Just as well, as it turned out.

AT THE SLOCAN CHIEF cabin, the group from Utah was enjoying their last evening after a truly fine day of skiing. They would be packing up and heading out the next morning. They weren't aware that their counterparts at the Silver Spray cabin were missing.

But a hundred meters away, in the little A-frame hut used by the custodian, Dave Heagy was monitoring the radio, ready to provide support, positive thoughts or just a human presence at the end of a radio phone.

Across the dark mountains at Silver Spray, Carrie Fitzsimons spent the long January winter night alone.

"I was her sole point of contact through the night," Heagy remembers. "She was a voice at the other end of the radio."

Heagy reassured Fitzsimons that he had been involved in a number of searches for missing parties, and they had always had a successful outcome.

"He was my comfort and my lifeline, and he assured me [Rob and the others] had the skills to survive, and to keep up hope," Fitzsimons recalled later. "I couldn't sleep. I went out and called for them many times, and screamed, and cried . . . and was as near insanity as I have ever been."

It's impossible to imagine what it must have been like for her.

{ 12 }

SUCH DEVASTATION

Saturday, January 3

DAWN ARRIVES SLOWLY to a mountain valley in early January. At first light, pilot Keith Westfall was at the helicopter base beside the lakeshore on the outskirts of Nelson, running through his pre-flight inspection. The morning was cool with gusty winds and clouds moving in and out, and the forecast was for deteriorating conditions and snow—lots of it. It was the kind of day when a chopper pilot would need to watch the weather very carefully. Lise Nicola's truck was parked outside the Nelson hangar, where she was scheduled to pick it up when she flew back with the last load that afternoon. Westfall, like everyone else, was holding to the hope that things would still go according to plan—that the missing Silver Spray party would be found alive and well.

The passengers on Westfall's first flight would be Sean McTague and Kevin Giles. Normally Giles would have taken over from Dave Heagy as custodian at the Slocan Chief for the upcoming week, but the two of them had decided that it made more sense for Heagy to remain at the cabin for now, while Giles helped with the search for the missing skiers. McTague and Giles were headed up to Silver Spray for a look around, and Westfall would fly Carrie Fitzsimons out from there. In the meantime, John Buffery, Marc Deschenes and Tom Van Alstine were driving to the Woodbury staging area, where the search and rescue volunteers from Kaslo were also assembling. Dave Smith, Terry Barter and Bela would arrive at Woodbury in a second chopper piloted by Duncan Wassick.

Westfall, McTague and Giles flew north over the lake and up the thickly forested slopes. From his back seat, with the windows fogged, McTague couldn't see much ahead. He could look down through the bubble window on his side, however, at the treetops and the ground. And as the helicopter rose up the side of the Woodbury Creek valley, he noticed a line of tracks in the fresh snow through the trees. Probably deer or elk tracks, he thought, although he would later wonder. The chopper cleared the tree line, giving the three men their first view of the open slopes of Clover Basin. Through clouds that partially obscured the terrain, they glimpsed a scene of vast destruction.

A massive avalanche had taken out most of the bowl, sending tonnes of snow to the bottom of the slope. The passengers in the helicopter could see the basin only in bits and pieces, but those pieces started fitting together to form a worst-case scenario. At the toe of the slide, on the surface of an enormous jumble of avalanche debris, they caught sight of what might have been a pack or a jacket. Evidence of a disaster that nobody had wanted to contemplate.

Giles used the radio to report in to the district parks office, giving area supervisor Steve Kent a pre-arranged code word so as not to alert anyone who might be monitoring that frequency. Kent would relay the information to the RCMP. Continuing on to the cabin, Giles and McTague got out on the snowy helipad and helped a distraught Fitzsimons climb aboard. Westfall then flew a circular route, avoiding passing over the avalanche site, towards the Woodbury Resort.

So it was an avalanche, after all. The disturbing news was relayed to those assembled at Woodbury. John Buffery, waiting for the helicopter bearing Carrie Fitzsimons to arrive, took a deep breath. He was now scheduled to go in on the next flight with Marc Deschenes to assess the scene and determine whether it would be safe for a search party to venture onto the avalanche track. While he prepared himself for the arrival of Westfall, the helicopter carrying Dave Smith, Terry Barter and Bela set down beside the lake. Smith went over to have a brief talk with Buffery, explaining that he was prepared to do a bombing run on Clover Basin if Buffery thought that was required after viewing the site. Smith had already put the gear he would need in his truck at the Nelson helicopter hangar. It would take him a couple of hours to fly back there, continue on to the government magazine where the explosives were kept, and then return to do the run, but the precaution would increase the safety of the rescuers. The victims had already been out overnight, so a short delay was unlikely to affect the final outcome.

When Westfall landed with Fitzsimons, Buffery and Deschenes immediately bundled her into Deschenes's truck to draw out any information that might be helpful in finding the missing skiers. Fitzsimons was confused and obviously rattled, so they kept the session brief. Leaving her with Van Alstine and the others, Buffery and Deschenes then climbed into the helicopter themselves. After a refueling stop in Kaslo,

Westfall headed into the mountains. Buffery recalls the dread he felt in the pit of his stomach. "This is probably going to change our lives," he thought.

Smith had rejoined Terry Barter on the beach at Woodbury, and they discussed who should head up the search effort on the mountain, now that it appeared one would be launched. They agreed to share the leadership until Smith was finished with his bombing run, after which he would be free to take over.

Up at the Silver Spray cabin, while waiting for events to unfold, Sean McTague and Kevin Giles had discovered first-hand how unstable the slopes were. The two had walked towards the edge of Clover Basin, intending just to look down into the bowl, but their movements remotely triggered a small avalanche far above and some distance away. "Oh boy, this really is shaky," thought McTague. The small slide hadn't put them in any danger, but it was a clear indicator of a precarious snowpack. Informed about this incident by radio, Smith suggested they stay close to the cabin.

Buffery and Deschenes peered intently out of the helicopter windows as Westfall approached the avalanche site, trying to see through the ragged veil of mist and blowing snowflakes. Although Buffery was a professional safety consultant, and certainly knew the importance of not placing rescuers at risk, this was going to be a tough call to make. "It's like, man, if there are people alive and you do blast the area, the chances of surviving that are none," he recalled. Given the limited visibility, it would be difficult to see from the air if there was anyone alive down on the avalanche path. Buffery had his fingers crossed that the slide had totally cleared the basin, leaving no hang-fire that needed blasting.

129

The helicopter cruised well above the avalanche site, dodging patches of cloud that made it impossible to assess the full extent of the slide. After several passes over the area, though, Buffery and Deschenes were able to piece together a more complete picture, identifying the crown, the enormous track and the vast area of debris piled at the bottom. It was hard to accept what they were seeing.

"It was a classic, classic avalanche path," recalls Deschenes. "An existing avalanche path that had obviously run before. Big alpine start zone, narrow track in the middle and big run-out at the bottom." This avalanche was so immense that it had spilled outside of the historical track and crashed through mature larches on either side.

From the steep, open slopes of the upper rim of Clover Basin to the broad flats below was well over a kilometer. The terrain of the upper part of the bowl was broken by several low-angled benches, or ramps. Towards the bottom, rock outcrops on either side squeezed the track through a chute about 150 meters wide, dotted with small trees, before it broadened out to about 300 meters across at the toe.

The avalanche had run virtually from top to bottom. The fracture line had sliced across the upper rim of the basin, well above where the skiers would have traveled. In fact, Buffery noticed that three separate avalanches had released around the rim of the bowl, flowing atop one another as they converged in the main track. While one of the smaller slides had made it only as far as an upper bench, most of the snow had packed enough energy to sweep down the slope onto the next bench, where more debris had accumulated, with most of the mass continuing on down, picking up more snow as it went. Where the bowl funneled through the chute, the cascading snow from all sides would have converged, blasting through the cliffs before spilling onto the broad run-out zone at the base. That was where most of the debris had ended up, including rocks, twigs, branches, stumps and even whole trees. It looked like a rubble field.

From the chopper, Buffery and Deschenes could see a ski track, a gliding traverse that entered the bowl from the direction of the Silver Spray cabin and disappeared under the avalanche path. The men scanned the far side of the avalanche path looking in vain for a ski track exiting the debris.

Down in the run-out zone, dwarfed by the epic scale of the scene, two figures were visible on the surface, partially buried. Those in the chopper searched for any sign of movement, seeing none. About 250 meters above those figures, where the avalanche track narrowed and steepened, was what looked like another body. Its descent appeared to have been halted by a small tree.

Three of the missing six skiers, apparently dead. It didn't seem real. And the others? Likely buried.

Although the slide had taken out most of the snow around the sides of the bowl, there were still some pockets of hangfire. Deschenes and Buffery knew it would be best for Smith to drop a few bombs to see if he could clear out these booby traps. "That was the hardest call," Buffery said later. "But it had to happen, and Dave probably knew that already. That's why he was poised and all ready to go."

The American skiers who had been booked to fly into the Silver Spray cabin that morning were notified that their week was canceled and their money would be refunded.

WHEN NELSON physician Anna Reid awoke that Saturday morning, she knew something was terribly wrong. She had sensed it, somewhere in her gut, the day before. Finally, with increasing dread, she phoned the Kootenay Lake Hospital in Nelson and learned that the emergency department had received a call from the RCMP a few hours earlier. There had been an avalanche in Kokanee Glacier Park, and the hospital was advised to be prepared for six trauma victims. Unfortunately, Reid knew very well who was in that group. Had she and Linda Kalbun not bailed at the last moment, might they have been among the victims, too?

Preparing to receive hypothermic patients with multiple traumas, the emergency room staff had started warming up blankets and stocking the fluid ovens. In a hypothermic state, the body's core temperature drops to dangerous levels. The various techniques used to treat this condition involve slowly warming up the core, perhaps by ventilating with warmed oxygen through a mask or by pumping doses of warm saline into the stomach, bladder or abdomen. Sometimes staff use a "bear-hugger," enveloping the patient in a puffy, quiltlike plastic blanket with baffles into which they pump warm air. It's important not to move hypothermic patients vigorously, as that might push cold blood that has pooled in the arms and legs into the core area, precipitating a cardiac arrest. Staff monitor the patients' hearts as their core temperatures gradually rise.

Six severely damaged patients would be a lot for the small emergency department to handle. Brian Moulson was the sole doctor on duty in the emergency department that day. Moulson, a family physician with his own private practice, also took shifts in the ward, as did most of Nelson's general practitioners. In his additional role as the hospital's chief of staff, Moulson was the one who had hired pediatrician Carrie Fitzsimons and anesthesiologist Rob Driscoll to work at the hospital. He juggled a full schedule, so he'd been grateful when Driscoll had generously signed to cover the emergency shift over Christmas, allowing Moulson and other doctors with young families to take the day off. Moulson had four children, and he was often seen on the nearby cross-country ski trails hauling the youngest behind him in a sled.

On this day, Moulson had only two nurses to assist him, but he was prepared to activate the hospital's disaster protocol if needed. That would call in almost all available hospital staff—physicians, nurses, specialists, and lab and X-ray technicians.

Emergency department staff generally have no idea who the incoming casualties are going to be. When an ambulance is bringing in a trauma patient from something like a motor vehicle accident or a skiing accident, paramedics phone ahead to report gender, age and vitals, but not much else. But in a small town, when the patient arrives at the hospital, staff may discover a friend or neighbor on the stretcher. As they made preparations to receive the avalanche victims, the emergency staff at Kootenay Lake Regional Hospital were hit by the realization that two of their colleagues, Rob Driscoll and Carrie Fitzsimons, were skiing that week in Kokanee Glacier Park.

BUFFERY AND DESCHENES had now joined Giles and McTague at the Silver Spray cabin. They were waiting for Dave Smith to arrive to do his bombing run. Instead, another helicopter unexpectedly appeared out of the valley, buzzing over Clover Basin and then landing on the helipad. It was the coroner arriving to take charge, bringing with him Tom Van Alstine, who had provided directions for the helicopter pilot. With his abrupt entrance, in rather poor visibility and without

133

warning, coroner Shawn Jestley immediately put the others' backs up.

"He stomped out of the helicopter saying, 'Who's in charge here? I want photos of everything before we move the bodies,'" recalls John Buffery. The searchers were incredulous. They were still in rescue mode. Of the six members of the missing party, only three had been accounted for. It wasn't beyond all possibility that the remaining three were alive somewhere.

"Dude, we're looking for people, we're not looking for bodies," Buffery thought to himself. "If it means digging them out and resuscitating them, that's what you're going to get before you get the coroner's photos. Sorry."

Deschenes was also biting his tongue. "To hell with the rules," he fumed silently. "Right now the weather is deteriorating. Let's just get these people out of here. We'll deal with the bureaucracy later."

But even in the mountains, sudden deaths must be reported to the Office of the Chief Coroner of the Province of British Columbia. So at five minutes after nine o'clock that morning, while the first members of the search party were getting their initial look at the avalanche site, the RCMP had put in a preliminary call to Shawn Jestley in Nakusp, a village some 60 kilometers northwest of the site. When the RCMP confirmed fifty minutes later that there were fatalities at the Silver Spray site, Jestley had hopped into a helicopter to head for the spot.

The coroner's job is to act for the deceased, to figure out, as Jestley describes it, "How come I'm dead?" In British Columbia, coroners are not necessarily doctors or medical examiners, as they are in some North American jurisdictions.

They are medical/legal investigators mandated to find out how, when, where and by what means a person died. Their role isn't to assign fault or blame, only to conduct a fact-finding mission.

Jestley had a job to do, but at that moment the searchers at the Silver Spray cabin were not interested in "How come?" They were trying to stay mellow, focused and clear. The plan was to make the site safe so they could get on the avalanche path and begin a rescue. And they weren't finding the coroner's attitude very helpful. As Buffery recalled later, "Boy, there sure was some friction between us." The five men badly wanted Jestley to go away. Instead, they explained who they were and what they were in the process of doing. Once he understood the situation, Jestley seemed to calm down. He climbed back into his helicopter to fly over the accident site and take photos, with Marc Deschenes along to help him understand what seemed to have occurred.

When Dave Smith arrived with Duncan Wassick, seconds later, to do his bombing run, the coroner's chopper was still buzzing over the basin. Wassick circled in a holding pattern while Smith watched impatiently, not sure what was happening and irritated by the delay. They had made the trip to Nelson, on to the explosives magazine and back in less than an hour. But already the weather was deteriorating; it was starting to snow. "We can't keep flying around in circles like this. We've got to get this thing going," Smith complained.

Once the coroner's helicopter had dropped Deschenes at the cabin and departed, Wassick flew low over the basin so that Smith could locate the figures the others had reported seeing. He and Wassick then discussed exactly where to drop the explosives to trigger releases. Wassick did a dummy run

135

over the designated locations to check the winds and make sure he could hold the machine where Smith wanted it. Then they did the runs for real.

Sitting in the back seat with his harness on, Smith lit the charges and dropped the explosives out the open door to their targets. "One away . . . Two away . . ." The bombs plummeted and sank into the snow. Smith kept time with a stopwatch so he would know how many seconds remained before the fuses burned down. Generally a 1-meter fuse will burn for two and a half to three minutes, depending on altitude and composition, giving the bombing team a minute and a half to complete the run, with plenty of time to clear the area afterwards. Smith and Wassick would watch from across the valley, looking for the boom or the puff of black smoke that indicated an explosion, then checking to see if the snow moved.

Sometimes the slope isn't ready to slide. But when it does, according to pilot Keith Westfall, it's a dramatic sight. "Suddenly you see a big crack in the snow and a whole slab will start moving. It's not just a bunch of snow like a snowball rolling down the hill. It actually pushes and builds in front of itself, because the top part coming down causes weight that makes the bottom snow shift a little bit, and it starts moving. So it's always building on itself, and the toe keeps running out farther as it pushes down. I kind of laugh at people who say, 'Oh, if I ever get caught in an avalanche I'll just ski out of it.' They don't have any idea."

That morning Smith dropped nine snow bombs, but most of the snow didn't move. The initial slides had likely taken the juice out of the snowpack. Smith did hit one higher snow accumulation, however, that crashed down onto the avalanche track, making it as far as one of the benches. You wouldn't have wanted to be underneath that one.

Smith wrapped up the bombing operation, satisfied that the slope was clean. At this point, he was free to assume the role of de facto search leader, so he gave the okay by radio for the searchers in the cabin to move onto the avalanche path for a beacon search. To communicate, they were using a designated radio frequency assigned to Provincial Emergency Program operations, so Smith could talk without the outside world listening in. Next he instructed a handful of Kaslo Search and Rescue volunteers to fly up from the Woodbury staging area to the base of the slide. There was still enough visibility to get down to the lake, although who knew how long that would last. Smith didn't want to bring in too many volunteers at this stage, increasing the potential for accidents with choppers coming and going in a tight spot. If a small initial response team could take care of the situation, that would save putting more people at risk.

Smith had Wassick fly him to the toe of the slide to await those coming in to help. The pilot set down the helicopter right on the deposit, which he would have avoided if there'd been other clear landing spots available. Landing on avalanche debris can impede a subsequent dog search, as the downwash from the rotor blades disperses scents or pushes them back down into the snowpack.

Some of the men who set out from the Silver Spray cabin had participated in real avalanche searches before, but nothing on this scale. Turning on their beacons to receive and traversing to the edge of the bowl, they looked down onto the avalanche path, which was intimidatingly vast, taking note of the major debris accumulations. The group split up from there, heading for different areas of the avalanche path to initiate hasty beacon searches. They would all eventually make their way towards the bottom.

Buffery found himself operating with a heightened sense of awareness, becoming ultra-focused and intent. He stayed high, starting his search along the route where ski tracks entered Clover Basin. At the point where the tracks disappeared under the avalanche path, a flat bench across the slope was piled with hardened debris that needed investigating. On the steep sections of the upper path, where it was scraped free of debris, the avalanche bed was hard and icy, making it difficult to hold an edge. Below him, Buffery could see Giles, Deschenes, McTague and Van Alstine spread out across the slope, searching over the deposits on the benches and checking the far side of the slide path for any sign of ski tracks leaving the basin. Most of the snow, however, had continued on down the slope to pile up at the bottom.

"Because of the sheer size and speed of the thing, a lot of the mass was able to make it farther," Deschenes remembered. "The toe is where most of the victims turned out to be, and that's typical in an avalanche path like that. Although there are short trees and old trunks that are broken from past avalanches, there aren't too many obstacles. So when you're caught up high, you likely end up at the bottom."

Smith, temporarily on his own at the toe of the slide, had begun the grim task of confirming fatalities. Although he knew Lise Nicola, he wasn't familiar with any of the other skiers. He found two men lying on top of each other. One of them appeared to have made a heart-breaking effort to dig out the other, but neither of them would have lasted for long. Down the slope from these two, Smith saw a hand sticking out of the snow. He dug until he could confirm that this person, too, was dead. All three skiers had incurred catastrophic injuries while being swept down the slope.

Through the broken cloud that hugged the valley below came the angry-hornet buzz of a helicopter. Moments later the chopper materialized and swooped to a landing on the debris. Terry Barter and Bela had come to join Smith. Barter turned off the beacons worn by the men Smith had found, so that the transmitting signals would not interfere with the rest of the search. Then he and his dog started a sweep across the avalanche debris in the rest of the run-out zone, searching simultaneously for radio signals and scent. Smith started searching with his transceiver, too, and he located another burial on the far side of the avalanche, at about the same elevation but 60 meters from the other three victims. He had just finished marking the spot when the helicopter returned with the first Kaslo volunteers, including Paddy Flanagan. Smith knew Flanagan was a steady guy, so he asked whether the SAR leader would be okay with digging for a dead body. "He said he was fine, so Paddy did most of the digging," Smith recalls. Shoveling through hard avalanche debris, Flanagan and a helper eventually uncovered a fourth body. That brought the total so far to four skiers found at the toe of the slide: Geoff Leidal, Rob Driscoll, Pat Von Blumen and Scott Bradley, as Smith would later learn.

Buffery, Deschenes, Giles, Van Alstine and McTague were still working their way down the slope. By now Barter and Bela had started heading up. As the Kaslo group continued to search in the run-out area, Smith, too, began climbing up the slope towards the spot where the avalanche track funneled through the chute and another bright jacket was visible. By the time Smith reached the site, Deschenes and McTague had already arrived from above. Mary Cowan's body had been stopped by a small tree. McTague turned off her beacon,

139

and he and Deschenes, with the help of Tom Van Alstine, who had also descended to the spot, carefully dug her body out of the snow.

Of the six people missing, four had been found at the base of the slide, and one higher up the slope. But Lise Nicola was still unaccounted for. The searchers had worked their way down the entire slide path. For whatever reason, if Nicola was buried somewhere in this massive avalanche, she was not transmitting a signal from her beacon. That meant they would have to probe for her body.

The thought of probing such an immense area was mind-boggling. It would be a mammoth task, and it could take days. Barter called by radio for further Kaslo Search and Rescue re-inforcements, but the pilots were watching the weather anx-iously. At any time the valley cloud could move up the slopes, and they would lose their visibility. The searchers might not get much more time on the mountain that day.

Dave Smith began organizing the searchers at the toe of the slide into a widely spaced probe line for a quick search along what seemed to be the avalanche's main trajectory. They progressed up the slope, pushing their probes into the solid debris. Other searchers spot-probed off to the side, where the fourth body had been found. Maybe they would get lucky there. But Nicola could also be buried on one of the upper benches where snow had accumulated. That was a huge area in itself. Where would they even start?

140   Smith had held off preparing the bodies for the flight out, thinking that the coroner would want to see them first. "I de-layed a little bit of time, and it came back to haunt me," he said later. When he realized at about three o'clock that the coroner probably wasn't coming, he got on the radio to

arrange for a helicopter to come in and remove the bodies. But by then, fog was rolling off the lake, socking in the valley below and gradually moving up towards the searchers. Several loads of people needed evacuating off the avalanche slope, and the two pilots were itchy to get moving. "When you have that many people out there, it becomes a bigger worry," pilot Duncan Wassick explained afterwards. "You have to make your decision sooner rather than later." It was time to pull the pin.

Smith called all the searchers back to the base of the slide to begin flying out. The group deliberated about leaving some of their number at the Silver Spray cabin to continue the search the next day, but the forecast was for deteriorating weather and a prolonged period of snow. There was no telling when the helicopters would be able to return to the site, and the searchers could be trapped up there for days.

Everyone realized that safety had to be the first priority. The searchers could place themselves in danger if they pushed the heroics too far, and in any case, there wasn't anything that could be done for the people who were dead. But nobody was comfortable with the knowledge that Lise Nicola was still missing. It was especially hard on those, such as Sean McTague, who knew her well. Was it good news that they hadn't found her, or not?

The two helicopters started ferrying loads off the mountain. Since it was now too foggy in the valley for the helicopters to fly down Woodbury Creek, the searchers were flown to Kaslo instead. The four bodies found at the toe of the slide were placed inside a large net sling from Wassick's helicopter. The sling would be attached to a cable suspended beneath the chopper. But the weather from below was moving up and closing in, and Wassick finally decided there wasn't time to bring out the net or to retrieve Mary Cowan's body, still higher up on the slope. There was barely time to get the searchers out. The last helicopter containing Terry Barter and Bela, the avalanche dog, lifted off from the site in the fading light at about four o'clock, just before the weather closed in.

Late that afternoon, staff in the emergency department at the Kootenay Lake Regional Hospital received a call from the RCMP telling them to stand down. There did not appear to be any survivors from the slide.

NEWS OF THE AVALANCHE rocked staff at the Canadian Avalanche Centre. The previous day there had been the avalanche that buried the snowmobile party near Sparwood, killing one man. That morning they'd heard about the fatal avalanche that had killed two skiers the day before near Mount Aylwin. Now there were a further five (potentially six) fatalities from Kokanee Glacier Park. That would bring the January 2, 2003, body count to nine. The death toll equaled that of the worst day for recreational avalanche deaths in Canadian history, which had occurred seven years before when nine helicopter skiers had perished in the Bugaboos. The center had also received numerous reports of close calls, nonfatal burials, recoveries, and what director Alan Dennis called "just-lucky-to-get-home agains." As he told a *Vancouver Sun* reporter, this avalanche cycle was a disaster.

Staff at the center prepared for the never-ending stream of reporters who would soon call needing a five-minute immersion course in Avalanche 101. After major avalanche events, the center usually allocated extra staff to work with the media, realizing that stories would go to air with whatever information could be assembled by deadline. "We try to help them and be a resource, because otherwise inaccuracies creep in," says Evan Manners. With every accident, there's a window of opportunity, a teachable moment to spread an educational message and, perhaps, make a pitch for more funding for the center's programs.

Although the avalanche center's public bulletin had warned about the potential hazard, staff couldn't help but feel, as they did every time someone died in a slide, that somehow they had failed. As Manners later said, "There's a real tendency here to take every tragedy personally, because we're working to prevent them."

SEAN McTAGUE was a close friend of Lise Nicola's. It upset and frustrated him that they hadn't been able to find her, that there had been no beacon signal to track down. He felt a personal obligation to look out for her interests. Back home in Nelson, he thought about the tracks he had seen on the forested slopes above Woodbury Creek during the helicopter ride up to Silver Spray. "What if Lise did get out—where would she be now?" he wondered.

The tracks hadn't really looked like human boot tracks. He was almost sure they were ungulate. It didn't make sense that they would be Nicola's tracks, either, especially given her height. Still, the thought unsettled him, and he couldn't let it go. What if Lise had survived the avalanche and started walking out, coming down the steep forest slope into Woodbury Creek? She might survive one night out in the snow, he figured, but probably not a second one.

After getting search leader Dave Smith's okay, McTague called the Kaslo Search and Rescue leaders to organize a few

143

searchers on snowmobiles to accompany him that night up the unplowed access road to the Silver Spray trailhead. From there the summer trail switchbacked up towards Clover Basin. The four searchers roared up the snowy road flanked by dark, steep valley walls, following the yellow beam of their headlights. They parked at the small parking lot where the summer trail started, pulled out their flashlights and tromped on foot up the creek to a small crossing, then started laboriously climbing through snow up the steep, forested slope. Smith had warned McTague to be very cautious since the snow was so unstable. Sure enough, the group didn't get far before encountering a slide path. It was too risky to carry on any farther. They stood in the dark forest, blowing a whistle, listening, calling out and listening.

{ 13 }

FLYING LOW

*

Sunday, January 4

WHEN DAVE SMITH woke up early Sunday, he saw that the snow was coming down in earnest. Damn. There wasn't a chance of flying until visibility improved. He'd really hoped for a shot at bringing out the bodies that morning. The longer the search was delayed, the more the pressure would build, as the news media gathered and friends and families waited anxiously. But the snowstorm had obliterated the mountains, and you couldn't even see across the lake. A blizzard virtually sealed off the West Kootenays from the outside world.

While Smith and the other search organizers from Nelson stood by, either at the helicopter base or at home near their phones, search and rescue volunteers from Kaslo waited impatiently at their command site at Woodbury Resort, hanging out in pickup trucks and campers. They had been joined by a dozen members of the Nelson Search and Rescue team. Lise Nicola had been an active member of that volunteer squad, and now her cohorts were champing at the bit to get up there and find her. Although her fate was still a question mark, hope was slipping away that she had somehow escaped being caught in the avalanche.

Nicola's friend Monica Nissen was among those at Woodbury waiting for a break in the storm. Nissen had heard about the Mount Aylwin slide the previous afternoon, discovering to her horror that two men she knew, Kevin Jewitt and Simon Lewis, had been killed. She and her roommate, Alison Lutz, had walked around Nelson to the homes of other friends to break the terrible news. At one of those stops, they had learned about another avalanche, this one at Kokanee Glacier Park. Nissen had immediately thought about Lise, whom she knew was up there. The two women frequently hiked, climbed and skied together, sharing their plans and dreams.

Nissen was a member of the Nelson SAR group, and she agonized over whether she should join the search for Nicola or find some other way to contribute. "On one level, of course I should join the search," she remembers thinking, "but this is my friend. Is it the right thing for me to do? How is it going to affect my head?" She and Alison ended up making pizzas all night. Nissen had decided that was how she could best support the rescue effort. But the next morning, when they delivered the pizzas to the Woodbury staging area, she decided to take part in the search, after all. As it turned out, her day was spent waiting out the storm, with plenty of time to think about her friend.

The first time Nissen met Nicola, she had found Lise intimidating. "Who is this woman, this pint-sized fireball who seems to have so much going on, and who pursues her sports so aggressively?" she'd wondered. Even though Nicola worked in largely male-dominated environments as a park ranger and a ski patroller, she seemed really strong and secure in herself. Nissen would find out that "like everyone, Lise had her vulnerabilities, but she really had passion, determination and drive."

Since their initial meeting, Nissen and Nicola had gone on many adventures in the mountains. Nissen couldn't figure out how her friend could have been caught in an avalanche. Lise was so conservative, and she always made such solid calls. "She wasn't crazy, she wasn't on the edge. She had a really similar risk tolerance to me," Nissen would later say.

There was finally a hint of an improvement in the weather by afternoon. Pilot Duncan Wassick decided to take a crack at flying up to Clover Basin to retrieve the bodies. Conditions were still brutal, and some questioned Wassick's call. But Dave Smith had faith in the pilot's judgment. If anything, Wassick was a pretty conservative pilot, he figured, and not interested in taking undue risks. "You don't know what you've got up there until you try," Smith later explained, "so it seemed a reasonable thing to attempt." Mountain weather is localized and changeable; while it could deteriorate, it could also suddenly improve and provide an opening. Really, the only way to know was to go check it out, always being prepared to turn around if necessary. They might get lucky.

The limits to safe flying are not clearly defined. Physical abilities such as depth perception and reflex responses play a role, and experience definitely counts. But every pilot is different. Some have a high tolerance for risk. Some are used to pushing the limits, and hence have a feel for exactly where those limits are. Pilots often get an indication of their comfort level with flying conditions by gauging their body's reactions.

147

A dry throat, shaking knees, spontaneous whistling—it's time to pull out and turn back. "The customer may or may not be happy with that," Wassick says, "but the thing is that you get home."

The purpose of the flight into the park was to retrieve the bodies of the victims. At least the billing situation was clear. It's not a moot point, with helicopters flying around the mountains at a thousand dollars or more an hour. The moment there are confirmed fatalities, an RCMP investigation becomes instead a coroner's investigation, with the RCMP assisting. But helicopter companies sometimes face a bureaucratic tangle in sorting out which agency is paying for their services.

"A classic situation is that you go out on a search and you find out the people are dead, and so then Search and Rescue won't pay for it because they only pay if you find somebody alive," says Wassick. "The coroner won't pay for it unless the people are dead, but that's only if you know they are dead when you go out. If you go out looking for them and you don't know they are dead, then it's a big squabble, and it's taken me sometimes six to eight months to get paid." Wise pilots have learned to document every flight, lift-off and landing so they will be better armed to handle subsequent paperwork. Accounting details are not something they want to worry about during the height of a search operation, however, while they are fighting snowstorms, encroaching darkness or dwindling fuel supplies.

It was decided that Dave Smith and Marc Deschenes would fly up to the avalanche site with Wassick, so the three men convened at the Nelson helicopter base. Once they were all strapped in, Wassick took off with a light load of fuel, so that the chopper would have as much power and performance as possible. It's easier to maneuver a helicopter—to stop quickly, back up or bring it vertically out of a hole—when there's less weight on board. As Smith recalls, they encountered "absolutely ghastly flying conditions," with such a low ceiling and such marginal visibility that Wassick had to skim the treetops all the way up the valley towards Clover Basin.

Trees give a pilot some ground definition in flat light. Above the tree line, however, in a snowy bowl with cloudy conditions made worse by fog patches moving through and no shadows to provide reference, the pilot literally doesn't know which way is up. His senses lie to him. Even seagulls have been observed flying out of clouds upside down. In the mountains, almost all the flying is vfr, Visual Flight Rules, which means pilots can't rely on instruments. If a pilot can't see the horizon, he can hit the ground and never see it coming.

Another problem with flying a helicopter in the mountains is that the craft's rotor blades can ice up. With their airfoil shape, rounded on top so that the air passing above moves faster and exerts less pressure than the air passing beneath, the spinning blades provide the lift that keeps a helicopter airborne. When the rotor is tilted, the blades provide the thrust that moves the machine forward or backward. But as the chopper flies through clouds, water vapor can condense and freeze on the blades. This will throw the rotor out of balance, and possibly cause the helicopter to drop out of the sky.

Wind can play a factor, too. In the mountains, wind flows rather like water would—over hills, down through valleys, swirling and eddying around rocks. Choppers work best flying into the wind. If the wind direction suddenly reverses, the pilot instantly loses the air speed that is part of his lift.

Despite the challenges, Wassick successfully arrived at Clover Basin and set down at the toe of the slide. Smith and

Deschenes leaped out into the deep snow. The weather was still a continuous threat, and although the men had brought gear to spend a night out in case of emergency, this would be a nasty place to have to shut the chopper down. They needed to work fast. There was just no possibility of retrieving Mary Cowan's body, which was still partway up the steep slope in an awkward spot. In fact, the men had already decided that they couldn't risk taking the bodies in the net all the way out to the highway. Instead, Wassick would transport the net off the treacherous part of the mountain by flying straight down to the parking lot where McTague and his group had gone by snowmobile the evening before. Dave Smith had realized that the bodies could be retrieved from there by snowmobile even if this nasty storm precluded further flying. Also, Smith didn't want to bring the bodies down to Woodbury, where the media would no doubt be gathering. He wanted to be as quiet about this operation as possible, transporting the bodies to an ambulance without them ever being on show. And he knew that if he could get at least the bodies of the four men down from the mountain, that would relieve some of the pressure that was building on everybody.

The four body bags were already inside the net sling, and the corners of the heavy net had been brought together and clipped into a big ring. Now Smith and Deschenes attached the ring to one end of a long cable. While Deschenes stood clear, Smith took up a position beside the load, holding the free end of the cable in his hand. Wassick lifted off from the ground, moved the helicopter into position over Smith and hovered there. With that deafening noise overhead, Smith reached to clip the cable into the load hook on the bottom of the carriage, checked that it was secure, then stepped out from under the machine. He moved to a spot where Wassick could easily see him, a bit to one side and in front of the chopper, and stretched his arms out wide—the all-clear signal. Wassick lifted off with the load dangling beneath him. Smith and Deschenes watched him go, hoping the pilot would make it back up the mountain for them. Regulations prohibited Wassick from carrying passengers while slinging loads.

Wassick didn't get far before he realized that the long cable line was forcing him to fly too high above the trees. He was rapidly losing visibility, so he was forced to turn the chopper around and go back. He radioed to Smith and Deschenes that he would have to switch to a shorter cable. There was a disadvantage to using the short line, though: when Wassick picked up or put down the net, he'd need to bring the machine closer to the ground, where there was more risk of it being caught in the middle of the snowball—the circular mini-blizzard produced by the rotor wash driving air down into the loose snow.

When he reached Smith and Deschenes, Wassick carefully set down the net on the slope and used an electronic device inside the cabin to disengage the cable from the chopper. He landed a short distance away to let the two men trade the long cable for a short one retrieved from the helicopter. Once that was done, Wassick took off and hovered again over Smith as the cable's free end was clipped to the underside of the helicopter. He left after the all-clear, tilting the chopper forward, clearing the trees and disappearing into the valley. This time the throbbing faded away, and the men were left in silence on the snowy mountain slope.

Wassick deposited the net carefully at the trailhead parking lot, then rose back up the slope to rescue Smith and

Deschenes. They clambered into their seats, and the three made a swift retreat back down to the lake. "We got out of there just before we iced up and fell out of the sky," recalls Smith.

Once back in Nelson, Smith had a tough decision to make. He had agreed to lead the search effort on the mountain. But all this new snow was accumulating on the slopes along highways in the region; he needed to stabilize those slopes before they started releasing. There was nobody else who could step into his avalanche-control job and take over.

The rescue at Silver Spray wasn't over, however. "We wanted to end it all for the families and everybody, so there was some closure there," remembers Smith. "But we didn't have Lise located, and we hadn't been able to get Mary Cowan's body out. There were two people who were still on the mountain. In the meantime, the storm was raging, and all my areas were lighting up." Smith had to find someone who could take on the daunting situation, a new site commander in whom he could place his confidence.

It was a relief when Tom Van Alstine, former head of safety at the local ski hill, agreed to take on the role. Smith knew Van Alstine to have a good sense of command and an orderly, methodical approach to making decisions. He would be just the right person for the logistics involved in this search, where the planners would be under a lot of pressure and would need to filter out background distractions. Van Alstine would be backed by capable help, since there was plenty of expertise at hand, and Smith himself would still be available in the evenings to provide advice.

So while Dave Smith turned his attention back to his highways job, Tom Van Alstine started to put into place the next phase of the search: finding Lise Nicola.

BOB HALL, a reporter at the *Nelson Daily News*, started working on the avalanche story early that Sunday morning. The *Daily News*, "serving Nelson and area since 1902," had its headquarters in an 1899, Late Victorian brick building on Baker Street. Hall had been there for three years, covering the city hall beat and any other stories his editor sent him chasing. The previous fall he had been assigned to interview the new pediatrician in town, and he'd been impressed by the young and friendly Dr. Fitzsimons, who even wore a nose ring. "She was super nice," he remembers. After the photos were taken and the tape recorder turned off, they'd chatted about her reasons for coming to Nelson, one of which was the skiing. Fitzsimons mentioned how lucky she and her partner, Rob Driscoll, were: they would be spending the week over New Year's up at the Silver Spray cabin. Hall wasn't a backcountry skier himself, but he thought the trip sounded wonderful.

Bob Hall's editor, Drew Edwards, had received a call early Sunday from a reporter at the *Calgary Herald* wanting information about a fatal avalanche in Kokanee Glacier Park. When Edwards roused Hall at home, Hall's first thought was, "Oh, my God, I probably know that person." The RCMP had not issued any names to that point, but the phones were already ringing with out-of-town media outlets seeking names and details. This would be Hall's first experience with a major international news story, and it would be an eye-opener.

In Vancouver that same morning, when reporter Ian Mulgrew clocked in to work at the downtown offices of the *Vancouver Sun*, his assignment editor informed him that he was headed to Kaslo to cover a fatal avalanche. Mulgrew and photographer Ian Smith drove out to Vancouver's airport and grabbed the first flight to Castlegar, the regional airport closest to Nelson.

Castlegar's airport is built on a bench above the Columbia River, surrounded by mountains. Incoming planes clear the mountain barrier and then plummet onto the runway; it's a little unnerving if you're not used to it. The airport has quite a reputation among North American pilots. Because of the terrain, pilots can do an instrument approach only to a certain point in the valley, after which they switch to a visual approach for landing. If there is low cloud and the pilot doesn't have sufficient visibility, he or she has to do a "missed approach" and head back up above the mountains. That happened all the time, especially in winter, and the region's government workers had learned that if they wanted to avoid a meeting in Victoria, the provincial capital, they should book an early morning flight that likely wouldn't end up flying.

With snowstorms smothering the West Kootenays, Mulgrew's plane couldn't land in Castlegar. It was rerouted to Cranbrook, in the Rocky Mountain Trench, about 140 kilometers by air to the east. As it turned out, the families of the avalanche victims, along with representatives from other media outlets, were also arriving in Cranbrook. Some of them had been rerouted as far east as Calgary, Alberta, and were now backtracking to Cranbrook. It would require a further four-hour drive west over an avalanche-prone mountain pass to get to Nelson and Kaslo. The weather was not making this easy.

Vince Nicola, Lise's father, was among those desperately trying to get to the accident site. According to a story by Mulgrew that ran in the *Sun* the next day, Nicola "stood stunned in the Cranbrook airport with his son, trying to find a way to get to Kaslo."

The *Vancouver Sun* team met up with a Vancouver-based television crew and arranged to share costs for a helicopter ride to the site. Not only would this get them to Kaslo faster, it might give them the opportunity to fly over the avalanche slope and get some aerial shots. The TV crew offered Vince Nicola and his son seats in the chopper, but they decided they didn't want to be the center of media attention. Instead, the two of them rented a car for the treacherous drive over Kootenay Pass.

The media gang took off into the snowstorm. "It was wild!" recalls Mulgrew, explaining that the helicopter pilot got lost a couple of times and had to keep dropping down out of the clouds to figure out where he was. "It was dreadful. We were buffeted; it was just roiling."

When they eventually came to ground on a helipad beside the lake in Kaslo, they were more or less the first media types to arrive. This turned out to be a coup, not so much to scoop the story as to nab the best rooms in the local hotel. The competing Canadian Broadcasting Corporation (CBC) television crew, arriving later, got inferior rooms with shared bathrooms down the hall.

Mulgrew walked up to the small RCMP office a couple of blocks away to find out what they knew. From Constable Jay Arnold he learned that a party of skiers had been caught by an avalanche two days before and that searchers on the site had recovered five bodies before deteriorating weather forced them to retreat. Four of those bodies had been brought down that afternoon to the valley bottom, but weather conditions had precluded bringing them farther. Another body was still on the avalanche path. The sixth skier was still missing. Further developments depended on the weather, and the forecast was not good.

Mulgrew filed his story. Ian Smith still needed a picture, but with the blizzard, there wasn't a chance of flying over the site that day. Instead, the *Vancouver Sun* crew headed to the nearby bar. Mulgrew bought a couple of rounds for the locals and regaled them with predictions about what Kaslo would look like when the rest of the media throng descended.

He was so right. Throughout the afternoon, reporters and media crews poured into town. "The little town of Kaslo was invaded by this small village of media. It was quite a spectacle," the RCMP's Jay Arnold recalls. The main street was taken over by satellite-linked trucks with cables snaking everywhere, reporters bearing big, furry microphones, and camera crews. Techies in brightly colored outfits scurried around, checking lights and sound levels.

"The Mounties were really quick to figure out that they should put together some kind of press release so they weren't answering the same questions over and over and over again," Mulgrew would later recall. Arnold ended up acting as full-time media liaison, preparing the releases and responding to the nonstop phone calls. He was dealing initially with print and broadcast reporters from Vancouver and Toronto, but then the calls started coming from much farther afield. The mayor of Kaslo, traveling in Japan at the time, saw coverage on television there. "We were burdened so heavily with media it physically tied me up, so I couldn't do anything else," Arnold recalls. He certainly didn't get much sleep. For a small detachment with limited manpower, the situation was overwhelming. "We really, really wanted to do our job and find these poor people, and to me it was quite obvious we didn't need to be giving updated news releases every half-hour."

But the story was clearly a hot one, feeding the public's fascination with a powerful and awesome force of nature. Danger, drama and five deaths—that was a lot of people to lose in an avalanche. The TV news people were drawn by the potential for footage of a big rescue effort, with its attendant adventure and derring-do. Some of them tried, unsuccessfully, to drive up snowed-in roads into the park to reach the avalanche site, which had locals shaking their heads in disbelief. There was also, at least at first, some indication that one person might have survived. "I think that added another element," Mulgrew recalls, "the idea of a survivor from something so horrific. That was a real riveting story people would be interested in."

Besides, early January is a slow time for news.

ACROSS THE PROVINCE, in the town of Port Alberni on Vancouver Island's west coast, it was raining. It rains a lot in Port Alberni, but it very rarely snows. As a result, Bruce McLellan, the RCMP dog handler with the Port Alberni detachment, hadn't had many opportunities to test his dog, Aslan, in real avalanche search situations.

McLellan and his canine partner had gone through all the training, though. Aslan had first learned to find his master when McLellan was hiding in a trench dug in the snow; next, he had found him when he was buried under a few centimeters of the white stuff. Then they had changed the game, so that the German shepherd sought for other people who were buried beneath the snow, learning to sniff out airborne scent from anything or anybody foreign to the scene. Every time Aslan found a snowbound victim, McLellan rewarded him.

That Sunday afternoon, after consultation with Tom Van Alstine, Nelson RCMP officer Terry Barter phoned to ask for McLellan's assistance with the search for Lise Nicola. McLellan jumped at the chance. In the absence of a beacon signal, dogs are the fastest way to find a buried body. In thirty

157

minutes, a well-trained avalanche rescue dog can search a hectare of avalanche path that would take twenty foot-searchers with probes four hours to cover. Given the size of this potential burial area, a second dog would most definitely be an asset.

McLellan packed up immediately, and he and Aslan started the long trip to Nelson: a ferry ride across to the mainland, followed by nine hours of driving over the mountain passes of southern British Columbia. He made good time, anxious to help with the search.

{ 14 }

IF IT BLEEDS, IT LEADS

*

Monday, January 5

JACQUELINE CASANO and her mother arrived at the Cranbrook bus depot before 6:00 AM, while it was still dark, to find the doors locked. The temperature was −16°C, so Patrick Von Blumen's sister and mother took refuge in a heated taxi. They had been having a nightmare of a time trying to get to Nelson. Their Vancouver-to-Castlegar flight the previous day was prevented from landing due to blizzards, so the pilot had flown on to Calgary. The airline had told the two women they'd be returned to Vancouver, but Casano put her foot down, so instead they'd been flown to Cranbrook. There, they'd overnighted in a greasy motel, and they were up early to catch the Greyhound bus that would take them the rest of the way to Nelson.

Finally, the big bus pulled up, and Casano and Siggy Von Blumen got aboard. The winter sky began to lighten as the bus cruised along the mountain highway, climbing up and over Kootenay Pass in the Selkirks. In spite of her ordeal,

Casano remembers being struck by the spectacular view from the windows. "The sun started rising, there was fresh snow-fall everywhere, and it was the most beautiful bus ride I've ever had, as awful as everything was."

When Casano and her mother arrived in Nelson, Pat's friends had a place lined up for them to stay, and they did everything they could to help the two women. Other out-of-town families were also making their way to Nelson, all trying to keep a low profile, well out of the media spotlight. The last thing they wanted was to have their grief headlining the evening news broadcast.

THE VANCOUVER SUN team's task on Monday morning was to get photographs of frozen bodies. "What people are looking for is the scene of the carnage, so that they can vicariously share in those final moments," says Mulgrew. "That's why we were there, and that's why the TV guys were there, and those were the only pictures that mattered. The police knew that, so then there was the cat and mouse game, because they, of course, didn't want us to get pictures of frozen bodies." The game, played out in an ongoing snowstorm, would involve helicopters, snowmobiles and ambulances.

A swarm of media people had already descended on the search headquarters at Woodbury Resort, where rescue volunteers were continuing to cool their heels while they waited for the snow to let up. Resort owner Terry Jones had set aside a room in his restaurant where grieving families and friends could keep warm, drink coffee and be shielded from the media scrum.

"It was just a media gong show. There were probably twenty reporters and at least four or five camera crews hanging around," recalls Jones. "They were in your face all the time. They were trying to get in here, and I said, 'Just leave the folks alone.'"

Adding insult to injury, the media people weren't spending money at the resort. "They didn't even buy coffee," Jones remembers with disgust. Because the rustic rooms at Woodbury Resort didn't come with phones, none of the media corps stayed there, opting instead for digs at the Ainsworth Resort, a few kilometers down the highway, or in Nelson itself. But they hung about the Woodbury Resort during the day, waiting for further developments, monopolizing the washrooms, and, it seemed to Jones, asking insensitive, unnecessary questions about the accident and its victims. "You know, they're dead. What info is there? It happened."

The weather prevented helicopters from flying up to the avalanche site, so plans were made for snowmobiles to bring out the four bodies that had been left at the trailhead. The turn-off onto the access road was just 4 kilometers up the highway from the Woodbury helicopter staging area. As snowmobiles gathered at the junction, along with an ambulance, the spot became a media magnet.

All for naught, as it happened. The snowmobile rendezvous turned out to be a bit of a decoy for the media—not really planned, but welcomed by rescue people nonetheless. The weather had provided a small opening after all, and a helicopter sneaked up the Woodbury valley to collect the bodies, flying back over the heads of the waiting camera operators to Kaslo. Once they realized what was happening, photographers and camera crews raced to Kaslo themselves, just in time to get shots of a bagged body on a stretcher being carried into the hospital there. The typical newspaper photo of this

161

moment shows at least four other photographers in the background trying to take the same shot of the same formless bag.

That night in Whistler, British Columbia, over 400 kilometers away, Geoffrey Leidal's mother, Carleen, would become increasingly angry as she watched the television news. "Here they are, showing body bags," she said later, "and you wonder if it's your own kid or not." Carleen Leidal hadn't been able to stop herself from watching the coverage of the avalanche that killed her son. But she couldn't understand why that kind of video footage was necessary.

When the four bodies were transferred to the Kootenay Lake Regional Hospital in Nelson later that day for postmortem examinations, the ambulance drivers avoided media scrutiny by pulling up to a back door loading ramp. The locals were beginning to catch on to this cat and mouse game.

For Dr. Brian Moulson, Monday was a demanding and difficult day. It began with an early call from the administration at Kootenay Lake Hospital, asking if Moulson could come in. Media inquiries had started arriving at the hospital the day before, as soon as it was discovered that the survivor, Fitzsimons, and one of the victims, her husband Rob Driscoll, were physicians there. Moulson had been drafted as the hospital's media spokesperson. He was a logical choice. Besides being chief of staff, he had been on duty when the hospital learned about the accident. He knew something about ski touring himself, having skied at the Slocan Chief cabin. He had also hiked into the Silver Spray area in summer and was familiar with that terrain.

That morning, the hospital administrator told Moulson that he had four reporters hanging about in the hallway. But before he had even finished asking the doctor to come in and

deal with them, the caller corrected himself: "Hold it—
there're six of them out there." Then another update: "No,
wait a minute, looks like there're another two arriving.
There're eight of them out there!'" By the time Moulson got
to the hospital and walked into a meeting room, three sides of
the room were lined with reporters and camera crews. He sat
down at the end of the table, where he would normally sit
while chairing a staff meeting, and microphones and tape
recorders sprouted before him.

When he had learned the previous day that he'd be handling media inquiries for the hospital, Moulson had spoken to
Carrie Fitzsimons and offered to deal with the media on her
behalf. They'd discussed what she wanted him to say and what
information she would be comfortable divulging. One of her
requests was that Moulson counter accusations that the Silver
Spray skiers were a foolhardy bunch. She felt newspaper, radio and television coverage had been very judgmental to date.
One of the RCMP spokespeople had been quoted as saying that
the group had perhaps been reckless, taking unnecessary
chances. "That was a bit of a delicate situation," recalls Moulson. "Without being critical of the RCMP, I had to try to dis-
count that as best I could, from what Carrie had told me."

When questions arose about risks, Moulson told the
assembled media, "This group was careful." He added that
the group was aware that unstable snow conditions in Kokanee Glacier Park meant a significant degree of danger. "The
avalanche hazard was high, and they were aware that it was
there. But [according to] my discussion with Ms. Fitzsimons,
it appears they were doing everything that a cautious and
prudent person in those situations and in that environment
would be doing."

163

Later, Moulson would explain the balancing act he had needed to execute at the media scrum. "I was trying to help [the media] understand the issues, but I was also definitely trying to protect Carrie, who was very fragile at that time." One thing that he managed to keep under wraps was the fact that Fitzsimons was pregnant. A reporter who heard a rumor about the pregnancy called Moulson the next day to ask if it was true, but when Moulson wouldn't comment, the reporter didn't use the information. "I felt that it was not part of the story," Moulson recalls. "It was just another tragic twist that would be used to sell newspapers."

In any case, the media had enough human drama to dress up the story. "You can only imagine what it must have been like to be by yourself, high in the mountains, in the dark, with six others that you've been with, and they've not come back from a trip," Moulson was quoted as saying by the Vancouver *Province*. "You can only hope that they maybe just got disoriented, dug a snow cave and were just waiting out the darkness. But your thoughts can go to the worst-case scenario, which is unfortunately what happened."

Another media conference was organized for later in the day by the RCMP in Kaslo. It was held in the government building across the street from the RCMP station, and coroner Shawn Jestley was there, along with Terry Barter. One of Barter's comments gave the media a new angle on the tragedy. It concerned a possible reason why Lise Nicola's beacon had not appeared to be transmitting and why searchers weren't receiving a signal. At first, this had raised hopes that Nicola might not have been in the slide. Now, as reported by the media, Barter hypothesized that she "probably survived the initial avalanche and may have been trying to find her colleagues when she was hit by a second slide." In that case, her beacon would have been switched to receive signals rather than transmit them. The possibility of Nicola's heroic sacrifice would headline Ian Mulgrew's front-page story in the *Sun* the following day: "Skier may have died trying to save colleagues."

Following the news conference in Kaslo, the *Vancouver Sun* crew bailed, as did many of their media colleagues, although some hung around to await further developments. The story was essentially over from the *Sun's* point of view. With snow forecast to continue for the next couple of days, there wasn't much potential for photos of bodies dangling beneath helicopters. "And we knew there was nobody coming down that was going to tell us anything," remembers Mulgrew. The paper could check in by phone with the RCMP and the coroner in a day or so. Mulgrew and his photographer headed down the road to the relatively cosmopolitan pleasures of Nelson for the night before heading back to Vancouver.

TUESDAY, JANUARY 6

Greg Stone traveled to Nelson from his home in Rossland on Tuesday, a drive of an hour and a half. Geoff Leidal's parents had asked him to deal with matters on their behalf. Carleen Leidal didn't fly, and the roads were bad. In any case, she felt she could be of more use providing support to her other sons. Stone readily agreed to help; he considered Carleen Leidal to be a second mother. Although he was five years older than Lumpy, they'd been close friends for two decades.

Stone remembered when Lumpy had first started tagging along with the riders from the Deep Cove bike shop. He'd been younger than the rest of them, but next thing they knew,

165

the punk was going faster than they were. Lumpy had thra-
shed down the bike trails with the older guys in summer and
joined them cross-country skiing in the backcountry of nearby
Mount Seymour in winter. Stone remembered how he and the
others had laughed when Leidal turned up with a snowboard
he'd built in woodworking class, careening and crashing down
the slopes on it. But he'd gone on to become a great boarder.

Leidal had been stoked on life, wanting to live it to the
fullest, and all of it at once. Anytime the two of them had got
together lately, the beer had flowed, the jokes had come thick
and fast, and they had laughed so hard they'd cried. And now
he was gone.

Stone had driven first to Kaslo, to collect Leidal's pack and
other belongings from the RCMP station, and had then made the
trip to the Nelson hospital morgue. Leidal wasn't the only one
he'd known in that room. Pat Von Blumen had been part of the
Deep Cove crowd, and Stone was also acquainted with Scott
Bradley. Through the local outdoor community, Stone had
even met Nicola and Cowan, who were still up the mountain.

Greg Stone didn't hang around Nelson. He did what
needed to be done as quickly and as quietly as possible, then
drove home to Rossland. Later, he would transport the ashes
to Geoff's parents in Whistler. That would be very tough,
he knew.

BOB HALL had watched as the media converged on the region, appalled by some of their intrusive behavior. As both a
reporter and a local resident, Hall found himself with a foot in
both camps—an awkward straddle. On the one hand, he felt
professional pressure to come up with a good story. On the
other, he would have to live with his neighbors, and himself,
long after the big guys blew out of town.

Hall knew that all the big-city reporters would be reading what the local paper had to say, so he felt he ought to have an inside edge on the news coverage. Not that he was personally interested in outdoing the big media outlets, "but I didn't want to look like a dumb-ass, either. My heart wasn't into it, though. I would have preferred to not do anything."

Hall had driven to the helicopter hangar to try to pry some information out of search organizers such as Tom Van Alstine, Marc Deschenes and Sean McTague, but he'd been escorted out the door. Unlike the out-of-town media, Hall didn't head up to the rescue base to wait for body bags to be brought off the mountain. He didn't go around knocking on people's doors or approaching the victims' families. "That's not stuff I could imagine myself doing," he said later, "because I can walk downtown and know 70 per cent of the people in this town by face, at least. How do you look people in the eye after being a complete jerk? The big media come in here and they have no connection, and then they'll just leave and go on to the next story. They leave us in their dust."

Hall's editor, Drew Edwards, a young man not long out of journalism school, was also taken aback by the callousness of many visiting journalists. In a subsequent editorial, he would write, "Like buzzards they descended on Nelson. The bodies, even buried under the snow, were too tantalizing to resist. The media smelled a great story and they came in droves." The *Nelson Daily News* editorial team felt that the bereaved families had the right to some privacy, but for many of the big-city news organizations, the only concern was for the story and who could get it first. "The feelings and emotions of those directly affected by the tragedy were not considered," Edwards wrote. The race to get the story, and to make it as dramatic as possible, led to sensational reporting, numerous errors and what Edwards later described as "a rapid decline to the lowest common denominator." But when he voiced his concerns to media colleagues working in Vancouver, "they treated me as though I had two heads."

Edwards had asked Hall to phone some of his helicopter contacts to see if he could pull strings and get above the avalanche site for a photo. However, the reporters soon learned that the RCMP had imposed a "no fly zone" over the site, so pilots refused to go there. "But had we done that and got overhead shots of some face on the mountain, we would have been heroes or something," Hall says today. "That's just the way it was. It makes me wonder if I'm a bad journalist, because I have absolutely no motivation to do something like that."

For his part, Ian Mulgrew didn't see that the media covering the Silver Spray slide had been any more aggressive than usual. "I don't know any people just waking up to the fact that newspapers are looking for pictures of dead bodies," he said later. "It's what we do for a living. Jeez, what do they see every morning when they pick us up or when they turn us on at night? If it bleeds, it leads, right? We can dress it up, but with all due respect, that's the nature of the game. I seem to recall that at the time, most of the media were being pretty sensitive about the locals. I've seen them be a lot worse."

The most sought-after person in Nelson, not surprisingly, was Dr. Carrie Fitzsimons. The out-of-town media had tried her office at the hospital and converged on the offices of the *Nelson Daily News*, wanting to know where she lived, since she wasn't in the phone book. They were after any information they could dig up about her, as well as photos.

"It seemed they needed to better one another, and that was what really bothered me, when they started prying into people's lives," remembers Hall, whose inclination was to shield Fitzsimons. This was especially so since Hall knew that Fitzsimons, like his own wife, was pregnant—information he didn't care to share.

Under the arrangement that newspapers such as the *Nelson Daily News* have with the Canadian Press, a news-sharing cooperative, local papers are expected to make their stories and photos available to other member newspapers. Edwards therefore supplied the Vancouver press with a file photo of Fitzsimons sitting at her desk, one Hall had taken when he interviewed her a few months previously. Edwards also provided a photo of Kevin Jewitt, one of the two victims of the Mount Aylwin slide, that had been given to the local paper by Jewitt's family. To Hall's dismay, the photos appeared on the front page of the next day's tabloid Vancouver *Province*. The huge headline beside Fitzsimons's photo, "New Wife Feared Worst as Night Fell," was followed by one that was almost as big: "Couple Had Been Married Only a Month When Avalanche Struck."

"It made me absolutely sick," Hall remembers. "The fact that it was my photo, and I would have to face this lady all the time, and she was probably going to think that I was exploiting something that she did in good faith. So I felt, honestly, sick to my stomach."

Carrie Fitzsimons would indeed be upset about the photo of her that appeared in the *Province*, and Dr. Brian Moulson would feel partly to blame. It was he who had encouraged her to make herself available to local reporters when she first arrived to set up her practice in Nelson. He had thought it would be good PR for the pediatrician. He could never have dreamed her photo would be used in the way it was.

THE UNRELENTING MEDIA attention of the previous two days had complicated the job of those planning the search effort. "It was a challenge trying to keep things organized and quiet enough to keep the press out of it as much as possible," recalls Tom Van Alstine. "They were like piranhas." The new search leader relayed his plans to the RCMP and left it to them to decide what to tell reporters.

The searchers knew that divergent messages would just create havoc, and it was better if the RCMP handled everything. They were also annoyed by the media's modus operandi, which they felt was aggressive and insensitive. Reporters had been phoning John Buffery at home; they had driven to Kevin Giles's house, hounding his wife with questions as she tried to leave for work. Marc Deschenes and other search organizers were pestered with questions about the avalanche every time they went down to the Nelson helicopter base. "I can't give you reliable information, because we don't know ourselves," Deschenes told one reporter after another. "There were no witnesses. Right now all I can tell you is that we're doing our best with the weather, we have to get in there and find everybody and get them out, and that's it. I'm not interested right now in finding out exactly what happened; that's not our priority. We just want to recover the bodies, just bear with us." But it was no use; the questions continued. Sean McTeague felt like punching the reporters at times.

At one point, a Vancouver television crew had come into the helicopter hangar trying to get an interview with Keith Westfall. Westfall, the pilot who had flown the Silver Spray group up to the cabin, had also taken part in the initial recovery effort. He was not interested in being interviewed, and he had already refused money to fly camera crews over the site.

"Nobody really wants to bring the vultures in, you know?" he later explained.

"We just want to ask you a couple of questions," the TV reporter said to Westfall, a small microphone in his hand. Westfall noticed that the accompanying cameraman was carrying his camera beside him like a suitcase.

"No, I'm not interested," Westfall replied.

The reporter persisted. "When you flew them in there, what were they thinking?"

Westfall just stared at him. What the hell did the reporter imagine the skiers would have been thinking as they flew in? That they were going to have a good time, probably. Nobody went into the backcountry to die.

Then Westfall noticed that the cameraman was swinging his camera around a bit. "That better not be on, you know," Westfall said to him. The reporter said nothing, and Westfall repeated, "I told you, no pictures and no interview here. And there better not be." At that point, Westfall remembers, the cameraman reached down and turned his camera off.

The searchers had closed ranks, making it their mandate not to talk to the media. When reporters did find individuals who would talk, those sources didn't necessarily know what they were talking about. One early television report erroneously stated that the avalanche had hit the Silver King chairlift at the Whitewater ski area (some 40 kilometers from the Silver Spray avalanche site), resulting in a barrage of phone calls to Whitewater's office. It was a relief for radio listeners frustrated by all this misinformation when Kevin Giles, one of the contractors who managed the Silver Spray cabin, and Dave Elliot, the owner of a Nelson outdoor equipment shop called Snowpack, were interviewed on the CBC, providing accurate information as well as insights into backcountry ski touring and its risks.

Andy Tyers, a Kaslo Search and Rescue leader, was one of those who later felt that media personnel could have been handled differently. "No one was telling them much, and so they were just making up what they could. They got a lot of wild stories," he says today. "We should have had a place for them to go instead of having them in our face all the time. They should have been fed more information. Our experience up until then was always to treat the press like the enemy, and that's not the way it should be. But every time you go on a search, you learn something. There's never a perfect search."

The RCMP did change their strategy after this incident, training specialized media liaison officers who could be brought to bat following a major accident. Eight months later, when another avalanche in Kokanee Glacier Park swept Michel Trudeau, the son of Canada's former prime minister, to his death, the force was far better prepared to handle the media invasion that ensued.

What really bothered many local residents was the same thing that had angered Carrie Fitzsimons: that some in the media seemed to have come looking for someone to blame. The coverage seemed determined to portray backcountry skiing as a dangerous, extreme activity, and those who participated in it as reckless yahoos. Reporters questioned the party's level of experience, their training and their judgment. The subtext of their stories questioned the skiers' decision to be in the mountains at all, given the risk of avalanches. Naturally, this didn't sit well with the local outdoor community.

"They don't freak out like that in an automobile accident," Marc Deschenes said later, "but people die regularly on the highways. But something like this in the backcountry. . . ."

"They want their pound of flesh and somebody to blame," concurred Terry Barter.

In fact, veteran Vancouver television reporter John Daly found the nonjudgmental attitude of most Nelsonites difficult to explain to his viewers in the big city. "I think they [the viewers] wanted a bad guy. They wanted someone to blame. A government agency, a touring company, a helicopter company that screwed up. They wanted to blame someone and they didn't get that," he said in a subsequent interview with the local *Weekender* tabloid. "Judging by most of the people we spoke to, friends and relatives of those who died accepted the risk that those people who went up to the glacier took. They understood that there was always a slim chance that something could go terribly wrong no matter what precautions they took. The people in Nelson seemed to understand that a lot better."

Most of the reporters covering the story didn't have a clue about what was involved in backcountry skiing. "Why were they out there?" they would ask. "Why didn't they have a professional guide? What were these people doing in the mountains during a time of avalanche risk?"

Local reporter Bob Hall could only sigh. "It's not like those [skiers] were naive fools out in the backcountry," he said later. Still, he couldn't really fault the big-city reporters for their lack of knowledge. "Those guys are more used to coffee shops than waist-deep powder."

{ 15 }

WAITING FOR THE WINDOW

Wednesday, January 7

WOULD THE SNOW never let up? Still at the Slocan Chief cabin, Dave Heagy wished it would stop. Under normal conditions, he would have come out of the mountains on Saturday, and Kevin Giles would have taken his place. But since Giles was involved in the search effort, it had seemed more logical for Heagy to stay and get the next group of skiers settled in. Now, with whiteout conditions preventing helicopters from flying, Heagy was stuck there.

It was tough being on his own, listening to radio coverage of the search but having no opportunity to talk about the events with colleagues, family or friends. He heard Kevin Giles and Dave Elliot being interviewed about the avalanche on the radio, and he didn't know how they managed it. "I was so emotional just listening to them, I couldn't cope," he remembers. On top of that, Heagy was dealing with a new group of keen skiers. "The avalanche hazard was not improving, and that didn't help my emotional state, because I had a group that wanted to get out and ski." When it snows big, people want to go after those turns.

Heagy wasn't the only one in the backcountry who was spooked. The news of Friday's fatal avalanches, followed by major snowfalls on an already top-heavy and unstable snowpack, was making a lot of commercial operators in the south Columbia Mountains very, very nervous. One heli-ski operator testing slopes by dropping explosives reported seeing sympathetic releases up to 5 kilometers away. Another operator chartered a helicopter at the first weather window to bring out his clients early, the first time he had ever taken such a precautionary measure. It was frightening up there.

At the Whitewater ski hill just south of Nelson, the bottomless powder seemed to be the stuff of which legends are made. Years later, people would still be talking about the amazing skiing that week. Among those enjoying the incredible conditions were the Americans who had been scheduled to fly into the Silver Spray cabin on Saturday. They had decided to stay in Nelson and go downhill skiing at the Whitewater ski hill instead. Actually, though, the hill was getting way too much of a good thing. The night before, an unprecedented slide had spilled onto a groomed ski run, taking out a swath of mature timber and shutting down one chairlift. During Wednesday's blizzard, an additional 55 centimeters of snow fell on the hill, bringing the storm total to 210 centimeters over eleven days. The staff had never seen inundations like that. Snow was accumulating dangerously on the ridges of a tall peak above the ski area, as well as along the ski hill access road, and Whitewater announced it would close down regular operations the next day in order to blast those slopes with explosives.

It seemed as if every slope in the region was in danger of shedding its load. Residents hardly dared stamp their feet because of what might come tumbling down on their heads. And the weather continued to sabotage efforts by searchers to return to the Clover Basin avalanche site to recover the last two bodies.

Search and rescue teams had been waiting to go up the mountain since Sunday. RCMP dog handler Bruce McLellan had arrived at the Woodbury helicopter staging area on Monday morning, ready for action, but the weather was no better, so the search team made plans to go in on Tuesday. Tuesday they'd prepared for Wednesday. But it was still snowing. Helicopters had made periodic attempts to fly up the Woodbury drainage to check things out, but poor visibility turned them back. By now, the Nelson SAR group had brought in their search and rescue trailer, which they parked at the base to provide a more comfortable command headquarters for searchers.

"How could we possibly do a rescue mission when we were still dealing with massive storms, and avalanche hazard was on the rise?" Marc Deschenes would say later, recalling the frustration. "People waiting, people wanting things to do, the press asking what had been going on, and all the rumors flying around as to whether Lise had survived, and why couldn't she be found, and why wasn't her transceiver working?"

The long wait was hard on everyone. Nobody expected to recover live victims, not anymore, but the searchers wanted to find Nicola, to end the uncertainty about her whereabouts and bring closure to her friends and family. They also wanted to bring down Mary Cowan's body. It was distressing to feel so useless in the face of all this snow.

It didn't help that the remaining media were waiting impatiently to document a valiant rescue attempt. Camera operators had been reduced to shooting footage of searchers putting on their boots. Some bystanders had a hard time understanding the delay. Why were the rescuers just hanging around? Why weren't they being action heroes, launching a dramatic rescue?

The search leaders understood the frustration. "It's really difficult to keep people in check sometimes," says Terry Barter, a veteran of numerous searches. "It's a hard decision to make, it's not a pretty decision, but you've got to go on the side of safety."

Tom Van Alstine concurs. "The bottom line with any kind of major rescue like that is understanding what the priorities are. Everyone's emotions tend to override the big picture."

The weather delay frayed nerves that were already stretched taut. Some searchers were anxious about what they would find on the avalanche site and how they would cope with it. Those who had taken part in the initial search had already witnessed death and had yet to process the troubling experience.

For those searchers who knew the victims, it was probably even worse. Sean McTague, as Lise Nicola's close friend, wanted to protect her interests, yet he could feel his own stress mounting day by day, taking its toll. "It wears down on you. It works on you over a period of time," he recalled. Every day when McTague drove to the helicopter base in Nelson, he saw Nicola's truck parked beside the hangar. One time he fingered "We love you, Lise" on the vehicle. Another friend drew a mountain skyline.

177

It's important for people involved in a search to be honest about their emotional well-being and to recognize their personal limitations. "You want to do as much for your friend as possible," Sean McTague says. "And yet you wonder, should you be here at all?" By Wednesday, when Van Alstine asked McTague what role he wanted to take in the search, McTague suggested he could be most useful handling radio communications from the Silver Spray cabin. That was the role he was poised to take on.

At least the days of nail-biting had been put to good use by Van Alstine and the handful of search organizers. In countless meetings at Dave Smith's department of highways office in Nelson, they'd refined a search strategy that would be implemented as soon as the weather gave them an opening. It was an operation of military precision that seemed to cover every eventuality.

"It was a huge amount of organization," Van Alstine recalls. "Meetings every night, meetings the next day. Plan A if the weather does this, or shoot into plan B if this happens, or into plan C." Once the weather cleared, the window of opportunity would be small. The potential burial area they had to search was huge. The rescue team would have to make efficient use of whatever time they had on the avalanche slope before returning clouds or encroaching winter darkness forced them off.

Van Alstine drew a map that divided the huge avalanche path into zones. Zone 1 encompassed the bottom half of the slide path—the run-out area as well as the chute above where Mary Cowan's body lay. This was the area where the recovered bodies had all been found. Terry Barter's dog, Bela, had already given it a quick sweep, and searchers had done a bit of probing in some possible burial spots, but it was still a likely place to find Nicola. Zone 2 covered the upper slide path, up to the elevation where ski tracks had been seen entering the avalanche path. It included several benches and ramps that were piled with avalanche debris. There could easily be a body buried on one of those benches.

Separate teams were assigned to zones 1 and 2, so that both areas of the slide path could be searched simultaneously. Each zone had a designated leader. All radio communication to the searchers would be channeled through these zone leaders to reduce the amount of confusing chatter on the airwaves. Each zone was also assigned a dog and a dog handler; a shovel-wielding volunteer to assist the dog handler and map the area as it was searched; a probe master to direct probing activities; three probe column leaders; and six probers plus a shoveler for each column. In addition, there were people designated to handle radio communications—McTague up at the Silver Spray cabin and a trained dispatcher down at the base headquarters, in the Nelson Search and Rescue trailer with its rooftop satellite dish. Kaslo's search manager, Andy Tyers, was made base commander, and Van Alstine would act as field search leader on the mountain.

In all, more than fifty searchers would be needed if the full strategy were implemented. In addition to the Kaslo Search and Rescue team, supplemented by Nelson Search and Rescue volunteers, Van Alstine tapped the rich vein of outdoor expertise in the area to pull together a group of people well versed in snow safety—mountain guides, avalanche professionals, ski patrollers, park rangers—to take on key roles. Ironically, several of the people contacted were unavailable that week because they were teaching avalanche courses.

A detailed flight plan was developed and distributed to key people. It specified who would fly to which zone, in what order, in which helicopter and with what equipment. "It was almost like an army operation," remembers Bruce McLellan.

179

"Everyone knew their role and where they were going to be. It was quite impressive how everyone worked together." Actually, there were a few communication glitches behind the scenes, but they never interfered in any substantive way with getting the job done.

Since dogs cover their ground most efficiently when there aren't crowds of people around to distract them, Bela and Aslan and their handlers were scheduled to fly up to the accident site on the early flights. A few other people would be on the mountain at the same time to support the dog search and set up safety procedures for subsequent stages of the operation. As more people and equipment were needed, the request would be radioed to the dispatcher down at Woodbury, who would then tell Andy Tyers, the base commander. Tyers would be supervising the comings and goings at four helipads on the delta. Probe column leaders would be standing by with their teams, ready to fly to their designated zones as soon as the call came in.

Three helicopter companies in the region were enlisted to help, so the group would have an A-Star, a Jet Ranger and a Bell 204, a larger machine used for heli-skiing and capable of carrying ten to twelve passengers, at their disposal. "If the weather changed, we'd have to get them out of there fast. We couldn't use the small ships," Barter later explained. Coroner Shawn Jestley would fly in a second Jet Ranger, and the RCMP would use their Long Ranger.

Even with the Bell 204, Van Alstine knew it would take an hour to ferry that many people to or from the mountain if the clouds started closing in again. Working out the logistics was a real challenge. The safety of the group had to be his focus, and he worked hard to maintain that perspective and stay disciplined. Because even after the plan was set, the snow continued to fall.

DOWNTOWN NELSON was still aglow with seasonal lights and displays, highlighted by a 10-meter-high Christmas tree. But the window of Snowpack, where Nicola had once worked, was stripped bare except for some poinsettia plants and a simple sign, "In Memory of Our Friends. January '98. Thinking of You . . ."

While the searchers waited out the weather, the people of Nelson were trying to come to terms with the recent tragedies. Not only were four of the Silver Spray casualties from Nelson, but the two victims of the Mount Aylwin slide also came from the area. The local hospice organized a grief support gathering for anyone in the community who felt the need to be with others to share his or her thoughts. As hospice volunteer coordinator Sam Simpson told the *Nelson Daily News*, "Basically the whole town is devastated, if not directly, then certainly indirectly. Just feeling a loss of this type has a pretty incredible impact on a small town because we are all so interconnected. You didn't necessarily have to lose somebody who is a close personal friend, but if they were a close friend of a neighbor or your kid went to school with their kid . . . there are just so many different connections. I had somebody say to me the other day, 'You just don't know whether to smile at anybody and say good day, because what if they are somebody who has lost someone?' That feeling sort of permeates the whole town."

At Rosemont Elementary School in Nelson, children in Debbie Zeeben's split grade five and six class had returned to their studies after the Christmas break to learn that their student teacher, Ms. Nicola, was missing in an avalanche. They were convinced that she would be found alive. She could hole up underneath a tree or something. She was skilled in avalanche safety and first aid, so if anybody could survive, it was Ms. Nicola. The class came up with all kinds of possible scenarios to explain what might have happened.

Nelson is a town where residents wait eagerly for the snow to arrive each winter, and many of them ski—whether at the local ski hill, along cross-country trails or in the backcountry. The downhill and cross-country ski lodges are a social whirl on weekends, a place to run into everyone from your neighbor to your dentist. On the morning after a big snowfall, a higher-than-usual number of people phone in sick to work or school—the unofficial "30-centimeter" rule. Some office workers manage to squeeze in a ski run before work, and before the lifts open, by climbing the slopes on foot. In addition to the usual cautionary lectures about drugs, sexual diseases, and drinking and driving, students at the high school receive talks about avalanche safety. Now, everybody who enjoyed the backcountry snow slopes was recalling times when they had been in potentially risky situations. As they reconsidered their responsibilities to their children and families, they were hit with a sense of their own mortality.

One counselor called on to assist with the psychological fallout was Nelson's Roland Perrin. As it happened, Perrin himself was an avid backcountry skier, out in the mountains every weekend, and he'd skied at Silver Spray in the past. He was on call with the RCMP and local search and rescue groups for critical incident debriefing whenever it was required, and he readily agreed to be available for sessions with volunteers after the search was completed. There would be two groups, one made up of those who had actually seen the bodies, and one consisting of those who had participated in the search but had not seen fatalities. The experiences and needs of the two groups would be different.

Confronting a violent death is significantly different from dealing with a normal death, around which our society has built in comforting regulation and ritual. In an accidental death, there is no regulation or ritual. There is terrifying disorder.

Witnessing such deaths can induce acute physical reactions, including nausea, disorientation, increased heart rate, hyperventilation, headaches and tremors. Rescuers may find their thinking impaired and have difficulty concentrating or remembering. They may experience anxiety, fear, depression, anger, guilt, grief or resentment. Some people simply go numb and withdraw. Many reactions may not surface until days or even years after the event, manifesting themselves as mood changes, sleep disturbances, feelings of isolation or apathy, flashbacks and nightmares.

Debriefing, a specific process led by trained mental health professionals, provides an opportunity for people to share the traumatic experiences they have just gone through. It helps to reduce the incidence of delayed reactions, which can affect even the most well-trained people. "It's not an issue of skill or knowledge," says Perrin. "Your defenses are struggling to cope with what you've been presented with emotionally."

It has taken time for emergency personnel to understand the importance of critical incident debriefing. The kind of people who voluntarily go out to save lives are often reluctant to seek help for their symptoms. And people whose daily jobs involve exposure to traumatic incidents, such as firefighters, police officers and other emergency personnel, can become desensitized to the effects of dealing with violent accidental deaths. Even for them, however, there are times when an event pierces this protective armor, and now many of these groups make debriefing a regular part of their routine.

For volunteers, the potential impact of dealing with violent death is likely to be much greater. In the case of the Silver Spray avalanche, many volunteers had known one or more of the skiers who had died. So setting in place a debriefing process would be crucial. There was a complication, however. A debriefing session is considered to be most effective when held between twenty-four and seventy-two hours after the traumatic incident. As Roland Perrin realized that the Silver Spray search would take several days, he had to decide whether to proceed with debriefing for the initial rescuers or wait until all the bodies had been recovered. That way, everyone could attend the same session and hear the whole story. Perrin decided to hold off.

The more prolonged the search, and the more people involved, the more complicated the logistics would be. In addition, there were the people affected by the deaths in the avalanche at Mount Aylwin. Perrin and his associates scrambled to be ready, arranging to bring in extra counselors from out of town.

THE CONTINUOUS bombardment of snowstorms finally eased on Wednesday afternoon, and a chopper made it in to pluck out Dave Heagy. Along with him were several members of that week's Slocan Chief group; as friends of some of the avalanche victims, they'd lost their appetite for skiing after learning about the slide.

Helicopters were able to fly to the avalanche site, too, but there was a familiar problem to be dealt with before the search could resume. More than a meter of new snow had fallen on Clover Basin over the past few days, and it was too risky to send rescuers onto those slide-prone slopes. Late in the day, Dave Smith flew back into the area to drop explosives and bring down the hanging snow. This time he dropped fourteen charges, releasing four slides. One was a whopper, running almost as far as the original avalanche. "It didn't have the same amount of mass, but it certainly would have smoked some rescuers," Smith recalls. "That gives you an idea how much the storm had dumped over those ensuing days."

To the east of the main slide path was a steep, loaded slope that wouldn't release despite the explosive encouragement. That hang-fire was marked on the version of the map Tom Van Alstine handed out to zone leaders in preparation for the search the following day.

The searchers were ready, and as prepared as they could be. But in the end, the best-laid plans would hinge on the weather.

{16}

NEEDLE IN A HAYSTACK

*

Thursday, January 8

"**I**T'S A GO!"

The phone lines were humming at seven o'clock Thursday morning as the search and rescue leaders enacted their call-out routine to contact volunteers. Finally, after five long days of waiting out snowstorms, they were getting a break. Temperatures had dropped, and a clearing trend was moving in from the coast. Patches of blue were visible among scattered clouds. The chopper pilots would be able to see the elusive horizon where sky met hard ground.

From their homes in Kaslo, Nelson and nearby communities, volunteers headed out on snowy roads towards the helicopter staging area at Woodbury Resort. As they drove along the lakeshore highway, they caught glimpses of the slopes across the lake for the first time in days. Snow was blowing off the ridge tops, a sure sign that it would be gusty up high.

Twenty-five-year-old Wren McElroy had joined the search party the previous day. She worked as a ski patrol at

Whitewater ski hill, but with two days off, she'd felt a strong pull to join the ongoing effort, even though she knew it would now be a search for bodies. She wasn't entirely sure why she wanted to be there, except that as a trained professional she had skills and capabilities to contribute. Van Alstine had welcomed McElroy as a strong addition to the core group. Raised in Nelson, she was a forest fire fighter during the summer, an avalanche instructor and ski patroller in winter, and an experienced mountaineer.

To be successful as a woman in the mountains, McElroy had discovered, you needed a really strong drive. It takes mental toughness to push through both the physical demands of the sport and the gender stereotypes suggesting you might not measure up. As a result, McElroy had found some women mountaineers to be very competitive. But one thing that stood out for her about her Mount Logan trip with Lise Nicola was their ability to work side by side, to pool their energy and support each other. She remembered one day in particular, when she and Lise had been carrying loads up a steep, snowy icefall between camps one and two. On the first carry, McElroy's pack had been really heavy and she had been slow, but Nicola had waited. On the second carry, it was Nicola's turn to be slow, and she had asked if McElroy wanted to go on ahead. McElroy remembered responding, "We're going up this mountain together, girl."

Perhaps, by helping with this search, she could be there one last time for Lise.

The searchers' main objective for the day was to find Nicola's body, which was likely entombed somewhere on a slide path the size of a few dozen football fields. As Tom Van Alstine later recalled, the task of locating one small body

187

without a radio signal was formidable: "Not knowing where she was, whether she was at the bottom, or the middle zone, or where? We didn't have a clue." The second task was to retrieve the body of Mary Cowan from partway up the slide path. They could expect the spot to be covered by further snowfalls and avalanche debris.

As the search and rescue volunteers congregated at Woodbury, Van Alstine, Marc Deschenes and Sean McTague flew in the A-Star directly from Nelson to the Silver Spray cabin, where McTague was dropped off to set up the radio link with the search and rescue trailer down below. Reliable communications would be crucial to the smooth running of the search operation. The logistics could get pretty wild when different parties used different radio frequencies, radios didn't have line-of-sight functioning, and choppers were coming and going in less than ideal flying conditions. McTague would act as air traffic controller, and he would also be able to relay messages to the base at Woodbury Resort from Van Alstine or the zone leaders on the avalanche slope if they couldn't make direct contact themselves on their hand-held units. He would keep a record of all radio communications.

After depositing McTague, the helicopter carrying Van Alstine and Deschenes flew over the avalanche track. Clover Basin was once again blanketed by snow. Like a white sheet placed over a violent crime scene, the new snow obscured the edges of the original slide path, smoothed over the old debris piles and erased evidence of devastation. Only a few orange stakes and flagging left from five days earlier indicated where bodies had been found in the run-out zone. Fresh avalanche debris generated by Dave Smith's bombing run the previous day had spilled onto parts of the track.

Satisfied from the air that the slope was safe enough for the search to proceed, Van Alstine and Deschenes had the helicopter pilot set down away from the toe of the slide. The machine descended gingerly into the cloud of swirling powder generated by the rotor wash. The pilot bumped the machine up and down a few times to firmly cradle the belly into the soft snow. When the next members of the search party arrived, one of their first chores would be to stamp out helicopter landing sites in each zone off the actual avalanche track. Helicopters have been known to tip over when one skid sinks deeper than the other into soft snow. Although the underlying hard snow of the avalanche debris would have provided a more solid pad, landing there would sweep away any scents wafting up through the snow and hinder the dog search.

As Van Alstine radioed the go-ahead to start ferrying in the first loads, a hazy sun was creating shadows on the slope. At the Woodbury base, the ground troops were waiting for the call to action, butterflies in their stomachs, anxious to get this over with. Andy Tyers, the base commander, received the okay from Van Alstine via the dispatcher in the Nelson Search and Rescue trailer, which was command central.

"Here we go!" thought Bruce McLellan as he watched Terry Barter and his dog, Bela, board the first helicopter along with Wren McElroy at nine o'clock. McLellan would be heading up with Aslan on the next flight. The dogs and handlers would spend about an hour doing an initial sweep of their respective zones and flagging any areas of scent before the probe teams arrived. Since Barter had done the initial sweep of the slide run-out zone, it was decided that the area should be searched by a fresh nose. Barter and Bela headed up to zone 2 with Deschenes, to sweep its upper benches and

189

low-angled areas. McLellan, arriving shortly afterwards, set to work with Aslan in zone 1.

With such a huge area to cover, even within his own zone, McLellan had to prioritize his efforts. Theoretically, a body could be buried anywhere along the slide path. But most observers of the slide's fracture line figured that virtually the entire slope had released in one go. The massive avalanche had probably slid with sufficient momentum to carry everything and everyone to the bottom, so the most obvious place to find Nicola was in the run-out area where the snow would have lost momentum. The fact that four other victims had been found there made it a location to target.

McLellan began directing Aslan's nose on a zigzag sweep over the expanse of snow. His dog was keen, but this wasn't one bit like his training sessions. Usually the surface of an avalanche path is frozen hard. In this case, almost a meter of the Kootenay's famous powder covered the avalanche debris. The dog had to leap over this snow, bounding up and down like an ungainly porpoise. McLellan was on skis, but not so the German shepherd. McLellan felt sorry for his dog and concerned, too. At this rate, he would soon have one tired puppy.

The second problem was that this wasn't a clean search. It wasn't like looking for one source of scent—a single smelly sock—in a field of otherwise pristine snow. The run-out zone was highly contaminated. The bodies of four skiers plus their belongings had piled up here. The tremendous forces involved had reduced many objects to fragments, dispersing the source of the scent. Rescuers had come onto the scene on Saturday, probing, digging and leaving more scents behind. Aslan had a lot of competing smells to sort out.

A dog's nose is truly amazing. It can detect scent a million times better than its owner's can. Airborne molecules stick to and dissolve in the animal's nasal cavity, which is rich in blood vessels, nerve endings and sensory receptor cells. The receptor cells send chemical messages to the olfactory region of the dog's brain. In general, a large or a long nose indicates a better ability for smell, and German shepherds are blessed with long noses.

How easily a dog picks up airborne scent in an avalanche situation depends on the denseness of the snow, the snow's water content, whether the scent has been diffused by wind or helicopter wash, and the number of competing smells on the surface. Often dogs don't arrive on the scene until after searchers have made their presence felt, packing down the snow, setting their belongings on top of a scent, dropping food crumbs or, worse yet, taking a leak in the search area. To help an avalanche hound cope with such real-life challenges, its handler incorporates into the training all manner of distractions that might lead a dog astray—dog biscuits, favorite toys and human and canine urine. To familiarize their dogs with the smell given off by bodies that have started to decompose, trainers can use a liquid product called "pseudo-corpse scent."

A dog will have no difficulty picking up a scent rising from 2 to 4 meters down. In previous searches, Terry Barter's dog had located bodies buried more than 20 meters below the surface. But the task is made more difficult if, as Aslan did, the dog has to nose through a meter of new snow.

With McLellan's encouragement, Aslan kept his nose to the snowfield. Meanwhile, further loads of key search personnel and equipment were arriving in zone 1. One member of this advance group was Cathy Grierson, whom Van Alstine had assigned as zone leader. A small woman with a signature blonde braid, she had a "take-charge" voice that she could unleash when required. Grierson was another Kokanee Glacier Park ranger who had known Nicola; she had also done stints as custodian at the Silver Spray cabin and was a first aid instructor. The personal connections upped the emotional challenges of her current role, and she had to put herself into soldier mode.

Grierson's main role, as she saw it, was to ensure the safety of the searchers. She felt confident that the key people organizing the search were of the same mind. "Safety was number one. I knew I was working with the best, and everyone had that focus. No one was wanting to be a hero," she remembered.

Grierson, Van Alstine, McElroy and others in the advance party got to work setting up the zone 1 search area—marking out the perimeter of the slide debris with orange wands, preparing the helipad and identifying escape routes exiting the avalanche track. They established a safe area, a sort of base camp and equipment cache, to the east of the run-out zone, up a short slope and protected by trees. This was where rescuers could wait when not actively searching on the avalanche track, eat or sip warm drinks, or urinate without contaminating the search area. At this point, nobody had any idea how long the search was going to take. With the large tarps and ropes in their equipment cache, plus stoves, food and sleeping bags, they could spend whole nights on the mountain if need be.

The equipment flown up to the site included shovels, probes, metal detectors, radios and extra batteries, first aid kits, transceivers, body bags and helicopter nets. There were three sets of colored wands tied with flagging tape: orange to mark the perimeter of the slide area, pink to signify any objects found on the slide path, and blue to indicate where the dog or a probe line found something under the snow requiring further investigation—a spot where shovelers should dig.

Paddy Flanagan, the Kaslo Search and Rescue team's leader on the mountain, had also arrived on an early flight. He was working with McLellan, mapping the progress of the search, helping to investigate and shovel when the dog showed an intense interest in one location (an "alert"). Aslan would dig vigorously and put his head into the snow, trying to locate the source of the scent, and McLellan would flag the spot with a blue wand. The first time the dog zeroed in on a spot, McLellan probed but felt nothing. With a shovel, he was able to find what had caught Aslan's interest. It was a puddle of blood where one of the bodies had been found three days earlier.

In Europe, where avalanche rescue dogs have been used for over fifty years, live recoveries are common. In North America, they are not. There isn't usually a trained dog close by, ready to leap into action, and a helicopter is generally needed to get a dog to the scene. Only once in Canada has a dog found a victim who was still breathing, a recovery that occurred near the Rocky Mountain town of Fernie two years after the Silver Spray tragedy. Several cases have been reported in the United States, including after a 1982 slide in Alpine Meadows, California, where a dog located a woman who had been buried for five days in a demolished building.

Looking way up the avalanche track, McLellan could just make out Terry Barter in his bright orange jacket, working with Bela across the benches in zone 2. From McLellan's viewpoint a kilometer away, they looked like two dots moving against the snow. Bela would be having an easier time of it than Aslan, spared the smorgasbord of contaminated snow and confusing scents found at the toe of the slide.

AT TEN O'CLOCK, leaving Cathy Grierson to oversee search efforts below, Tom Van Alstine and Wren McElroy started climbing on skis up the track towards Mary Cowan's body. They had both known the young woman from her time working at Whitewater ski hill, and McElroy had gone through Nelson's L.V. Rogers High School a couple of years ahead of Cowan. They knew her body was wedged behind a small tree where the avalanche had funneled through rocky cliffs. The steep slope there was dotted with dozens of small trees, many with torn limbs or shattered trunks. On an active avalanche path, trees never have a chance to grow to maturity. The spot where Cowan was found might have been obvious to the initial searchers, but with a meter of fresh snow now blanketing the site, which tree was it? Cowan's radio beacon had been switched off when her body was found, of course. So Van Alstine and McElroy probed and probed, encountering logs and stumps, wondering each time whether they might be making contact with a body.

Up in zone 2, Barter and Bela had completed their initial sweep, finding nothing of note, and Barter had radioed down to Woodbury for the first probe line to come in. Helicopters were flapping overhead, bringing equipment and further searchers. The commotion was distracting for McLellan's dog at the base of the slide, but the handler kept Aslan on task. "I wasn't in Vietnam, but it probably felt something like that, with the helicopters coming in and out," he would later speculate.

194

Monica Nissen was one member of the probe team that landed high on the slope in zone 2. With some relief, she realized that she had been assigned a low-probability area to search. Once the helicopter disappeared back down the valley, she looked across the mountain terrain and found it eerily quiet and peaceful. "It didn't look like a disaster zone, just like a snowy slope," she recalls. Nissen was shocked to see how large the avalanche had been. "It was almost incomprehensible, looking across, to see how big the fracture line was. And from where I was standing, I couldn't even see the bottom. It was huge."

RCMP investigator Jay Arnold took advantage of a lull in traffic to fly to the Silver Spray cabin. He wanted to catalogue the belongings left behind by Driscoll's group in preparation for returning those items to the skiers' families.

Suddenly, unannounced, there was a sound like a giant angry hornet, and the large Bell 204 appeared over the trees, heading for an apparent landing on the zone 1 helipad. Grierson was thrown off guard by this unexpected arrival. Had anyone in her zone requested extra volunteers or equipment? What was going on? Her radio crackled with questions, but in moments the big machine was landing and Grierson couldn't hear through the noise anyway. She watched a team of eight eager searchers climb down from the chopper and crouch beside the skids, ready for action.

As it turned out, there had been a glitch in communications; a pilot who had been unable to transmit on the SAR frequency had nevertheless signaled the base personnel to load the helicopter and had taken off. The result was a chopper full of searchers flying to the zone 1 site before they were needed. After sending a radio message requesting the base to hold off on sending any more reinforcements, Grierson had to decide what to do with the ones on hand. The important thing was not to interfere with the dog's sweep of the avalanche debris. Grierson showed the new recruits the orange wands that marked the perimeter of the search area, as well as the designated escape route and the area assigned for activities such as resting or eating. She gave them instructions to stamp down the escape routes. "I thought I communicated clearly," she said later. "Then at one point I turned around, and there's somebody right on the debris eating a sandwich!" The volunteer was a ski guide who should have known better, and Grierson found it awkward having to pull rank and reprimand a colleague. She did it, anyway, ordering him to get his food and his pack off the search area. She could sense the other searchers thinking, "Okay, we're not going to mess with her."

McLellan helped to keep the new recruits busy. As Aslan continued to indicate scents, McLellan flagged them with blue stakes and called in others to spot-probe or dig in those places. The searchers uncovered skis and gloves as well as human bone, stumps, branches and mature trees—it was amazing what was under that avalanche. A phenomenally destructive force had been unleashed on this slope, demolishing everything in its track.

"A lot of people were absolutely blown away by the force of the avalanche and its destructive capabilities," said Van Alstine later. "Not only to avalanche paths and trees that are in the way, but to human bodies."

Even experienced avalanche professionals came away with new respect for the unbelievable power of a snow slide. "I didn't really understand that until I saw it," recalled Grierson. "Holy shit! The size of the trees that it pulled out! I think that was one of the most powerful things to me—the depth, the power and the destruction of an avalanche, and to know it can happen to anyone."

The depth of the snow piled up at the toe of the slide was really brought home to RCMP investigator Jay Arnold the following summer, when he returned to the area. By then the snow was gone, of course. But he could still see the flagging tape that searchers had tied to nearby broken trees to mark the locations where bodies were found. The pieces of tape were now about six meters off the ground.

WREN McELROY and Tom Van Alstine were still probing several hundred meters up the track. At 10:40 AM, McElroy had found one of Cowan's skis, flagging the location with a wand. It was noon before she dug out the second ski. By that time, Van Alstine had radioed to Marc Deschenes up in zone 2 to come down and lend a hand. Deschenes had been involved in the initial discovery of Cowan's body, and he recognized certain trees and terrain characteristics at the site. "It's right around here somewhere,' " he told them, but when it came down to an exact location, he, too, was confused. He and Van Alstine kicked themselves for not putting flagging tape on the little tree beside the body. They probed for another half-hour through the waist-deep powder before Deschenes finally found Mary Cowan's body at 12:38 PM. Wren McElroy carefully held Cowan's head and helped lift her body out of the snow.

197

NOW IF ONLY they could find Nicola. Aslan had continued to push through the deep snow. Nelson Search and Rescue volunteer Murray Springman had been skeptical about how much the dogs would really contribute to the search. But watching Aslan at work, he was amazed. "It's just incredible how they can pick up the scent of a ski pole, for example, five days later. A ski pole! What scent would a ski pole give off?" he later marveled.

Springman was manning a shovel behind the probe line. McLellan had asked the volunteers in zone 1 to undertake a probe search to investigate what he thought were some likely areas, judging from where the dog had indicated scents or where other clues were found in the snow. In earlier planning, the search organizers had decided that the probe columns should use a technique called "three-hole step probing," a compromise between a coarse and a fine probe. Consequently, the volunteers were now lined up side by side, facing upslope. The distance between them was such that with arms outstretched they could just touch fingertips. Each carried a vertical probe.

"Pole down—left!" called the column leader. At the command, the volunteers poked their probes into the snow just to the left of their boots, angling them at 15 degrees. They felt for obstructions, pushing the poles down about 2 meters, well into the solidified snow. "Pole up! Pole down—center!" They probed into the snow straight down in front of their feet. "Pole up! Pole down—right!" This time they probed to their right, again angling the pole 15 degrees. "Pole up! Step forward!" The entire column stepped forward one pace, about two boot lengths, and the sequence began again.

198

It was slow, methodical work, and the area they were searching was a miniscule part of the immense avalanche field. What were the chances of finding a body this way? It was like looking for the proverbial needle in a haystack.

"Pole down—center!" Each time a searcher felt her probe make contact with something beneath the snow, she wondered, "Is it the ground underneath? Is that a body or something else?" It was hard to tell. Whenever it happened, the probe was left in place, and the searcher was handed another to use while moving forward with the column. Shovelers hustled to the marked spot to find what the probe had encountered. Frequently, it was a false strike, a stump or a rock.

Grierson was not participating in the probe line. She needed to be able to stand back, to keep an eye on the larger picture. McLellan and Paddy Flanagan were still sweeping with the dog, and the probe line was slowly working its way up the slope. Higher on the track she could see Van Alstine, McElroy, Deschenes and Laura Adams, another local avalanche professional, working together at the spot where Cowan had been found. Tiny figures were moving across the snow in zone 2, far above, occasionally swallowed by clouds. She wondered how long the weather would cooperate as she felt the minutes ticking by.

TOM VAN ALSTINE was also wondering. More than three hours had passed since they'd started searching. "Okay," he thought, "we've probably got another hour. If we don't find Lise by then, we'll have to back off and start moving people out." The days are short in January, and it could take an hour to get everybody off the mountain.

McLellan was having the same thoughts. He knew that Aslan was the key to their success, but he noted how worn-out his pooch was looking. Although McLellan felt the pressure, he tried not to lay it on the dog by showing his anxiety.

199

The German shepherd was more than just tired; he was also becoming discouraged. During Aslan's training sessions, whenever he found a buried article of clothing his reward was to tussle with it. McLellan would grab one end, Aslan the other, and they would play tug-of-war with a soggy sock. But this time there was no reward. McLellan wasn't even letting Aslan dig down to find the source of the scent, not wanting the dog to use up all that energy. People with shovels could do the digging more efficiently, once the dog showed them where to dig. So Aslan was pulled away time and again and urged to continue nosing through the deep snow. McLellan could sense the dog's frustration, and he wished he'd thought to bring along a substitute reward.

Aslan indicated again near the bottom end of the run-out zone, and McLellan poked a few times at the spot with his own probe. Was there something there? He wasn't sure, so he turned to the probe line, suggesting: "Maybe just dig there, because I can kind of feel something." Then he moved on.

Murray Springman and a second shoveler dug through the snow. What would it be, another stump? But this time it wasn't a false strike—it was a backpack. Nicola's backpack. With it was her radio.

They were getting closer. Some of the probe-line volunteers felt queasy, and they forced themselves to take slow, deep breaths. Most of them had never before seen someone who was dead. Already many knew they wouldn't be sleeping that night. A lot of them had known Lise Nicola; it was hard to find anyone in Nelson's outdoor community who didn't. But they worked to focus on the task at hand.

Nicola's body, being heavier than her pack, would likely not have been carried as far. One would expect to find it up the slope from her pack, so that's where the probe line now concentrated its sweep. The line moved slowly uphill, three-hole step by three-hole step, a small platoon of men and women poking poles into the snow. One person in the column was Tim Rippel, an Everest climber and guide, and yet another example of the wealth of outdoor talent in the region. He had been guiding for an out-of-town heli-ski outfit when the avalanche happened, but he'd returned in time to participate in this search on his day off.

Rippel moved up the slope in unison with the column. One of the other probers felt an obstacle under the snow, but it turned out to be a false strike. Then Rippel's probe encountered something else, deep down. He left his probe in that spot and was handed another as the line continued to move forward. Murray Springman was one of those who dug at the location of the probe, clearing away new snow and then moving rock-solid chunks of avalanche debris. About 2 meters down, he caught a glimpse of yellow. A yellow parka. It was the body of Lise Nicola, a sweet woman whose laugh had been infectious. She was buried deeper than any of the others had been, and farthest down the slide path, but in the same area. Five days earlier, the widely spaced probe line had missed finding her. The time was 12:50 PM.

Paddy Flanagan halted the probe line, and most of the rescuers were asked to clear the area. Cathy Grierson came forward to help. "The less people exposed to this, the better," she thought. Like most of the victims of this avalanche, Nicola had died not of suffocation but of catastrophic injuries. Grierson and several others carefully and gently dug the body out of the snow and placed it in a body bag. The memory would stay with them long afterwards.

And that was it. With both bodies recovered, the six-day search was over. A relieved Van Alstine gave instructions to Sean McTague to start sending for helicopters to evacuate the searchers at the upper end of the slide.

Down at Woodbury, Andy Tyers had been about to send another probe team to zone 2. Now he switched gears and prepared to receive people coming down from the mountain instead. The searchers who were still on standby, as some of them had been for days, were told they could go home, with no further explanation. They looked at each other, nonplussed. After all the nervous anticipation, all that waiting and internal preparation, how could they get in their cars and go home to a normal afternoon? It just wasn't possible. Meanwhile, coroner Shawn Jestley, who had been waiting at Woodbury, was headed up to the avalanche site in a helicopter to take possession of the bodies.

Nicola's body was carried to the zone 1 helipad and loaded into Jestley's chopper as soon as it arrived. Rather than waste precious time bringing Cowan's body down to the helipad, the searchers had prepared a makeshift landing site near her body. There wasn't enough flat surface to land the skids, so the coroner's helicopter did a toe-in to the incline, placing the front of the skids on the snow and using power to hold them against the slope as the chopper hovered in place. Once searchers had placed the second body bag in the chopper, the helicopter lifted off.

202

Load by load, the searchers flew down to Woodbury. When Cathy Grierson arrived, she found the scene unbearable—people were standing around talking not far from where the coroner was presiding over the bodies of two people she knew. It seemed . . . she wasn't sure of the right word . . . tacky? The helipad where Nicola and Cowan lay was closed off to the public and the media, with a guard to prevent anyone from intruding. The helicopters bringing down volunteers and equipment were using the other landing pads. But still, she wished they would hurry up and get the bodies in an ambulance and out of there.

Wren McElroy agreed to help identify Nicola for the coroner. When she unzipped the body bag, she saw Nicola's long eyelashes covered in snow. Nicola's transceiver, still strapped against the side of her chest and zipped under two layers of clothing, was switched on but not set to the "send" position. That's why it was not transmitting, and why rescuers had not been able to pick up a signal. It was a question to be investigated later.

McElroy thought of a photo taken of Nicola on Mount Logan at 4500 meters. They had been stuck in their tents at that camp for a week due to bad weather. But one evening about ten o'clock, despite howling 90-kilometer-an-hour winds, the sky had been incredibly clear. While McElroy, Derek Marcoux and Lise Nicola sat outside, pink light spilled across the surrounding mountains. The St. Elias Range stretched into the distance, and they could actually see all way to the ocean. What a place to hang out, they'd thought. It had been a glorious moment.

The search was finally wrapping up, putting to an end what Van Alstine figured was the most stressful week of his life by far. Searchers were packing up and driving home, often in silence, emotionally drained. The reverberations from this avalanche would unsettle the community for a long time, and they would mark a watershed in the lives of many who had been involved.

"It was a real eye-opener for me," remembers Marc Deschenes. "Despite all the training and all the preparation you do year after year, I don't think you're ever ready for something like this."

Bruce McLellan felt the same way. "It was a big search," he would say later, "a big learning experience for me. I'll probably never be in a big one like this again. It's not one you forget."

Up on Clover Basin, the search and rescue volunteers had all been flown out, and the RCMP helicopter was bringing out the last load. Van Alstine, Barter and Bela had been scooped up from the avalanche path, and now the chopper set down briefly at the cabin to pick up McTague. As rays of afternoon sun pierced the clouds and lit up distant slopes, the Long Ranger took off, swooping over the deserted bowl, dropping into the timbered valley and following Woodbury Creek to the lake. Two hours later, the light slipped away from the mountain slopes and the long winter night began. The windows of the little Silver Spray cabin were dark. Snow rested gently on the slopes, like the softest of goose-down duvets.

Fresh mountain powder, the stuff of which dreams, and avalanches, are made.

REVERBERATIONS

SEAN McTAGUE spent much of the rest of the winter of 1998 as custodian at the Silver Spray hut. He thought of Lise Nicola whenever he was up there. "In the voice of the mountain winds, in the warmth of the cabin, I feel her presence," he wrote. He set aside several pages in the black-covered Silver Spray cabin logbook with its duct-tape label in memory of those who had died in the January 2 avalanche. Friends who subsequently flew or hiked up to the cabin added poems and messages.

"Lise—you told me this place was one of your favorites, now having finally come up here, I can see why!"

"Lumpy, I finally made it up here to say my goodbyes . . . You will always be my inspiration to make the most of each day. 'Go big or go home.'"

"Rob—missing you on the peaks, runs, rivers . . ."

"Mary, it seems that I can't go dancing without seeing you out there on the dance floor, smiling your beautiful smile.

Keep dancin', sister, and I know that Pat will be there dancing with you."

"They all would have said, 'Don't worry about us,' 'Just remember our smiles' and 'Think about our love' so with time we won't worry anymore, we will remember their smiles and always feel their love."

The deep snowpack instabilities that had contributed to the tragic events of January 2 lingered. Every time someone dug a snowpit, the facet layers were revealed. But as it happened, there was never the particular combination of variables present to produce another major avalanche event that winter. The intense snowfall during the week following the Silver Spray slide triggered an avalanche cycle that actually improved the situation in the region by cleaning out many of the treacherous, overloaded slopes. Skiing conditions in the backcountry were pretty good for the remainder of the season. "But it was a long winter," remembers McTague.

In the immediate aftermath of the avalanche there were numerous memorials, funerals and wakes. At a gathering honoring Lise Nicola, Deb Zeeben's eulogy compared the promising student teacher who'd spent time in her classroom to a brisk morning breeze blowing over the mountaintop. Alice Weber and two other friends played guitars and sang Tom Petty's "Wildflower." Out of respect for Nicola, none of the food contained garlic. Hundreds of mourners packed a service in North Vancouver for Scott Bradley. At a memorial organized by friends for Pat Von Blumen and Mary Cowan, with photographs, bicycles and mementos hanging from the walls, Jacqueline Casano talked with humor about growing up with the bundle of energy that was her younger brother, with his surfeit of confidence and charisma. "You just have to see pictures of him, with that gleam in his eye," she said later. "He was definitely a presence."

Greg Stone transported Geoff Leidal's ashes to Whistler and stayed there for the wake. Leidal had always told his mother that, in the event of his death, she should throw a party, and over six hundred people turned up at the pub at the base of the ski lifts. Some had known Leidal since kindergarten. Two different women approached Carleen Leidal claiming to have been Geoff's first girlfriend. It was a wild evening even by Whistler standards. "I think it's their way of coping," said Carleen Leidal later. You can lose a lot of friends in a place where people challenge nature.

Brian Moulson stood watch outside Rob Driscoll's memorial service in Nelson to prevent any media from intruding, but the only reporter who turned up was there to pay his respects. Inside the church, Driscoll's long-time climbing partner and friend Bruce Fairley gave the eulogy. He concluded it with a bit of whimsy. "In my mind's eye I have a picture of a conversation going on in heaven right now between St. Peter and the Angel Gabriel, as St. Peter studies his clipboard and says to Gabriel, 'Say, Gabriel, that fellow over there, the one with the ponytail—I don't remember letting him in through the gates.'

"And Gabriel replies, 'Well, no, St. Peter, he actually climbed over the gates in a moment when you had your back turned. But you know, we've checked him out; he's all right, and we've decided to let him stay, anyway.'

"And Peter continues, 'I see, Gabriel, but what's he doing? What are all those ropes, and what have the angels got on their backs?'

"'Well, Peter, those are backpacks the angels are wearing. It seems our new friend is organizing something of an expedition. He's got a few of the more timid angels together, and he's going to take them out flying. He wants to take them higher than they've ever flown before. You know, I think it might be a great adventure. Maybe we should go along.'"

Driscoll had been one of Fairley's favorite people to spend time with in the mountains. "He just wanted to devour as much mountain country as he could," Fairley remembered later. "Rob had a lot of friends, and I think the reason I got asked to do the eulogy is that they thought I was the only one who could get through it without completely breaking down. And when the service started, I thought, 'Oh, no, I can't do this. I can barely speak.'" Fortunately, he was able to pull it together.

Following the service, Carrie Fitzsimons was approached by a lanky man with a gentle presence and a familiar voice. He introduced himself, and the moment was emotional—it was Dave Heagy, who had talked with Fitzsimons across the mountains during that long, difficult night.

In a tribute entitled "The Embrace," published in the *Nelson Daily News* a week after the tragedies at Silver Spray and Mount Aylwin, Jason Draginda, the owner of Nelson's Ripping Giraffe Snowboard Shop, wrote about his friends who had been killed in the accidents on January 2: "With the rest of the world looking on and asking questions like, 'Why were those people in the backcountry at all?', this I sum up by saying, 'If you don't know, you wouldn't understand.' Until you spend the time outside in the fresh air whether it is on your bike, skis, kayak, snowboard, it might not make too much sense. The craving for the interaction with nature is the most single driving force in almost everyone that I know. If they do not get outside and breathe, sweat, laugh, hoot or holler, they are not the same people. The sparkle in the eyes or the smile on their face is the indication."

Lise Nicola's grieving friends made their own forays into the mountains to honor her spirit. Alice Weber, Monica Nissen and two other women skied up to the top of a ridge near Whitewater ski hill carrying in a backpack a bottle of Nicola's homemade loganberry wine. With the peaks stretching out in front of them, they toasted their friend and had a picnic on the snow. It was the kind of girlfriends' ski day Nicola would have loved.

One month after the avalanche, Wren McElroy stood on the stage of Nelson's Capitol Theatre in front of a full house. It was the night of the Mount Logan slide show. "Our team started out over a year ago as six; tonight we are five," she began. Describing Nicola as "a very special person who lived with compassion and humble strength," she and her fellow climbers lit a candle onstage to represent Nicola's spirit and energy before launching into a multimedia presentation with music and several projectors, celebrating their time on Canada's highest mountain.

IT WAS SOME TIME before those who played supporting roles in the tragedy felt their lives settle back into balance. "It was like being on a roller coaster for a month," Brian Moulson remembers; in addition to his usual busy schedule, he dealt with grieving patients, media enquiries and funerals. Counselor Roland Perrin found himself working twelve- to fourteen-hour days to help people cope with the psychological fallout. In a decade of experience with critical incidents, he

209

had never been involved in one that required so much of his time and energy.

After returning home to Rossland from Whistler, Greg Stone couldn't bring himself to go skiing. Instead, he packed up and flew to Australia for six weeks of windsurfing. When he arrived home again, he knew it was time to get back on his skis. Climbing a local peak called Old Glory, and shaking with emotion as he jumped onto the slope from the top, he skied down the north face.

When Jacqueline Casano realized that her two children had developed a fear of skiing after their Uncle Pat's death, she immediately signed them up for ski lessons. And when Scott Bradley's sister, Lori Byrd, who had been pregnant when her brother died, gave birth to a boy, she named him Scott. "My brother would have been a fabulous mentor and uncle," she says today, imagining her children mountain biking and hanging out with her brother. "I miss him every day, but of everything, I feel saddest about that."

On Valentine's Day, six weeks after the avalanche, reporter Bob Hall's wife, Janice, gave birth to their son in Kootenay Lake Hospital. It was an induced labor, so Dr. Carrie Fitzsimons was on hand to attend to the infant.

"I'm sitting there with my wife delivering my child," Hall recounts, "and my heart is just breaking because here's this lady who's sitting there watching me, the husband, helping my wife deliver the baby. And when she delivers her baby in three months from now, she's not going to have her husband beside her." He suspected that Fitzsimons lumped him in with the rest of the media vultures, yet here she was helping his family. It brought home to him the awkwardness of being a small-town media person.

Three months later, when Coroner Shawn Jestley came out with his report and recommendations on the Silver Spray avalanche, Hall's editor asked him to phone Fitzsimons to get her reaction. Hall balked. "I said no, I'm not going to phone the lady. If you want the story, you do it." It became a big debate in the newsroom, but in the end Hall prevailed.

The coroner's report into the deaths concluded that safety precautions at the cabin had been satisfactory, and that those in the Silver Spray group "were aware of the reported high avalanche hazard and poor snow stability but chose to ski regardless. . . . The party, as a whole, made the choice to ski where they did, when they did, among themselves and with full knowledge of the prevailing conditions." Jestley noted that Clover Basin is known avalanche terrain. On January 28, he had flown over the Silver Spray cabin again, this time accompanied by avalanche experts who gave the opinion that the area lacked terrain that could be used safely in poor snow stability conditions.

Accordingly, B.C. Parks, Kootenay District, commissioned a reassessment of the avalanche risk at Silver Spray cabin. Based on that report, which was released in September 1998, park officials decided to close the cabin for winter use, despite protests from local skiers. The report suggested that there was even some small risk of the cabin itself and its immediate vicinity being hit by a slide in a five-hundred-year cycle. The closure continues today.

The RCMP investigated the issue of Lise Nicola's transceiver, hoping to shed light on the question that lingered unanswered long after the search wrapped up. Why was Nicola's beacon set in the wrong mode? Initially, there had been speculation that she might have survived the initial avalanche, then changed the setting on her transceiver from "send" to "receive" as she attempted to locate her buried companions. According to that theory, she was caught by a second slide. But in that case, one would expect the transceiver to still be outside her clothing, not zippered under two layers. Also working against that possibility was the fact that Nicola's body was deeply buried and found farthest down the slide path. That indicated she might have been the first caught. The trauma to her body suggested that the slide that engulfed her was immensely powerful. That too made it more likely to have been the initial one, which probably propagated dramatically around the top of the bowl.

So what had happened? In her rush to join the group at the last minute, might Nicola have accidentally turned her transceiver to the wrong setting? Could she have done the standard transceiver check before the group headed out for the day, with her beacon set to receive, and then neglected to switch it back before tucking the beacon away? Another suggestion was that, during the trauma of the avalanche, Nicola's beacon received an impact that knocked the switch out of position. Some helicopter skiing companies had reported problems with that particular make and model of beacon, saying that an impact could bump it over to receive mode. When the police investigated Nicola's transceiver after the accident, however, there was no sign of trauma to the unit; it seemed to be functioning properly.

"Unfortunately, it's typical in something like this accident that we don't get a lot of the answers," says RCMP investigator Jay Arnold today. "They're still out there."

Families, friends and those in Nelson's outdoor community had other troublesome questions following the Silver Spray avalanche. In private conversations and personal soul-searching sessions, people wondered how the accident could have happened. Why was a smart, experienced group of skiers on an avalanche slope like that in those conditions? How did they misjudge the danger? Was it only in retrospect that it seemed like such a bad judgment call? Might *they* have made the same decision?

Professional backcountry ski guides, such as John Buffery and Marc Deschenes, have jobs that require them to find the right balance between giving clients the skiing experience of a lifetime and keeping them alive. They have to make decisions that are more conservative than those they might make when out skiing with friends. And every guide involved in the January search wondered what decisions he would have made if he'd been guiding a group at Silver Spray in those conditions.

"I run that through my head a lot," says Buffery today. "I keep thinking, if it had been me and my group, what would I have done?" If a professional guide had been there, he speculates, that person could have made the unpopular decision and said, "No, we're not going out there," taken the rap and had people grumpy at him. "Because that's the role you take sometimes," he explains.

"It's very exposed terrain. It's intimidating, really," concurs Deschenes. "I look at that and try to imagine, okay, I've got a group up that I'm guiding, and I'm responsible for their safety. We've got a shitty week. Shitty weather, shitty snowpack, high hazard . . . what am I going to do with these people? Just about nothing, really. With good friends, it's one thing. But when they are clients you have to pull back more and not cross that line you draw for yourself."

The group at Silver Spray did a lot of the right things and made decisions based on their best assessment of the risks. But with the fresh storm snow, Clover Basin must have looked

213

very scary that day, Dave Smith figures. "They were hanging above that major path. The exposure must have been huge. Your hair almost curls up there, because you know you're right in the line of fire. Did they look down there and see those trees and imagine what would be the consequence if they did get nailed and then carried right down? Those are the kinds of things that you need to be asking all the time."

The details of the Clover Basin slide can never be fully reconstructed. But avalanche professionals try to learn from these tragedies, so they are constantly piecing together what might have taken place.

"After looking at photographs taken by one of the skiers, it appears that they entered the area one at a time, skiing onto a flatter bench," says Tom Van Alstine now. "One can only speculate what triggered the avalanche. It could have been the added weight of those last skiers joining the group. Or possibly it was as they started to traverse one at a time across the main slide area that the avalanche released."

Marc Deschenes also pictures the Silver Spray group crossing the slope, perhaps one at a time, aiming for a fairly flat spot. "You get there, and one person stops and waits for the others. The second arrives, the third arrives; now we're grouping up. The fourth arrives, the fifth arrives, and then suddenly 'Whumph!' That extra fifth person, that extra weight, was critical enough to cause the collapse. Spread out or not, I suspect there was a large 'whumph' and an immediate propagation along the weak layer—propagating upslope above them, finding the weak spot, and releasing the avalanche initiation point. And game over."

John Buffery, for his part, uses the accident as a teaching tool in his avalanche courses. After students have learned all of the technical stuff—snow metamorphosis, slope stability tests and such—he hits them with the reality of the Silver Spray avalanche. "It brings people to understand the realness of it, the bigness of it. Not just lovely fluffy crystals falling out of the sky. It's a mass in motion."

Buffery runs his students through snow and weather data for the days before the slide, right up to the observations recorded by Lise Nicola in the weather log that morning. He gets them to note the lack of snow early in the season, the crystallization and faceted layers within the snowpack, and the subsequent snowfalls. The skiers were headed for the Woodbury trees, he explains, a smart choice of terrain. As they crossed the basin, they were probably spread out. They probably thought they were safe, out of the reach of slides that might run. But they were skiing over potentially treacherous layers of faceted grains. "When you're on facets on flat benches, that's what collapses," he tells students. "That wave of collapse just runs up the slope to where the tension is, and then the tension releases. I bet it came like a freight train, pretty fast."

While there was never an opportunity to do a detailed fracture line profile of the fatal snow slide, Buffery had managed, during the initial day of the search, to take a very hurried look at the shear line along the upper flank. "I just really quickly stuck in my pole and felt around," he recalls. At that point, on the 38-degree slope, the depth of the slab was about 120 centimeters. Buffery estimated that it was probably a lot deeper higher on the slope. He could see that the avalanche had slid on a hard, frozen crust. On the exposed staunchwall (the vertical wall of snow that remained where the slab had sheared off), Buffery noticed a layer of loose, faceted crystals, about 30 centimeters thick, sandwiched between that hard crust and a more cohesive layer of snow above. On top of that cohesive layer were 60 to 80 centimeters of new snow from the most recent storm. The deposit there was much deeper than Nicola had recorded at the cabin, likely due to the addition of windswept snow deposited by the previous night's strong north winds onto this southerly lee slope.

In his courses, Buffery keeps his recounting of the avalanche factual and dry. He doesn't give an opinion about the decisions that were made, but instead shows his students the data. "I just say, This is what I saw, and this is what we did."

He has recounted the facts of the Silver Spray avalanche numerous times. And every time he does this lesson, he gets choked up. "I've seen big avalanches," he says, "but I've never seen devastation like that."

YEARS WOULD PASS before Alice Weber regained the confidence she had felt that summer she had climbed with Nicola in the Bugaboos. Her friend had been careful and thoughtful, so for her to die in an avalanche made Weber acutely aware of dangers you can't predict, of unknowns beyond your control.

Wren McElroy, too, found herself becoming far more conservative in her backcountry skiing. The power of the avalanche had amazed her: "Seeing big mature timber be ripped down and broken in half . . . we think we're so solid, but we're really so fragile, and that became clear to me." It was sobering to realize that Nicola, whom she would not have considered a risk-taker, could be killed in such an avalanche. This new awareness has shaped the perspective McElroy brings to teaching her avalanche courses.

After Nicola's death, Lise's parents gave Monica Nissen their daughter's climbing rack. Whenever Nissen was on the

216

rock after that, she felt as if she were climbing with Lise. She ended up becoming a teacher, like Nicola, sometimes even teaching in Deb Zeeben's classroom at Rosemont Elementary. Her dream, like Nicola's had been, is to share her passion for the outdoors with young people, and she initiated a project to bring avalanche education into the schools. "It comes down to Lise," she says today. "Her life and death have had a huge effect on me. It's all about that day."

Several permanent legacies now exist to honor the skiers who died. North Vancouver's Capilano Golf and Country Club awards a trophy in Scott Bradley's name each year to a worthy, all-round young golfer. Once a keen junior himself, Bradley had been hugely generous with his time and friend-ship to other young players. The Cove bikers named a North Shore trail after Pat Von Blumen. The mountain biking com-munity in Whistler commissioned the "Spirit of Lumpy," a 32-centimeter-high bronze trophy that depicts Leidal crouched on his mountain bike and descending a rough track. It is presented each year to a young mountain biker who ex-emplifies the enthusiasm that Leidal showed for the sport. At the 1998 Winter Olympics, held in Japan two months after the avalanche, Whistler resident Ross Rebagliani dedicated his gold medal in the first-ever Olympic snowboard race to his friend Lumpy. (The medal was stripped from Rebagliani when he tested positive for marijuana but subsequently rein-stated.) Trees were planted along Nelson's lakefront pathway in memory of Mary Cowan and Lise Nicola. Scholarships and bursaries in the names of Robert Driscoll and Lise Nicola provide financial support to students at Selkirk Community College in the West Kootenays. A small alpine lake at a back-country skiing lodge northwest of Kaslo is now named Lise Nicola Lake.

Carrie Fitzsimons gave birth in the spring of 1998 to a son, Robert, a carbon copy of his father in both looks and behavior. She continues to live in Nelson, where she is a highly respected and appreciated pediatrician. Although she was eventually able to move on with her life, she found herself much more fearful of outdoor activities that carried with them a degree of risk. She has never again gone backcountry ski touring. "From my perspective as the one left behind, I don't think the joy and the thrill is worth the pain," she said following the accident. "I would never do that to my son."

Vince Nicola made it up to the Silver Spray cabin in early July, three and a half years after the accident. Immediately following the search, pilot Keith Westfall had flown Lise's father, along with her mother and younger brother, over the site. Now, on this summer day in 2001, Vince Nicola hiked with friends up the trail that crosses the rocky meadow and tumbling creeks of Clover Basin. He and his companions carried a heavy plaque honoring the six victims of the avalanche, as well as the equipment required to bolt it to a boulder in the basin. They chose a spot beneath the towering spires of Sunrise Mountain, looking south onto a spectacular view of peaks and valleys.

It was midweek, and the group had the Silver Spray cabin all to themselves. As Vince Nicola lay in the bed that his daughter would have used, thinking about the avalanche, there was a violent thunderstorm. Then it stopped, the sky gradually lightened, and the sun came up over Sunrise Mountain. "I'm not really that much of a spiritual person, but it was very emblematic," Nicola recalled. "It was almost as if she was trying to connect with me, like she was saying she was okay."

218

"My daughter is my inspiration," says Nicola today. "She was probably my harshest critic and my best friend." Thinking of her has spurred him to become more involved in the outdoors, and it has helped him pick himself up after the tragedy. "Lise would have wanted that; she would have demanded that."

NO ONE WILL EVER KNOW exactly what happened in Clover Basin on the morning of January 2, 1998. A Molotov cocktail of terrain, snowpack, weather, human judgment and plain bad luck conspired to produce a fatal avalanche that swallowed up six remarkable people on a bluebird day when life seemed imbued with promise. Some mornings in the mountains are so dazzling your heart could burst. But life is tenuous, and avalanches are tricky. In seconds, everything can change forever.

How fine the line
Between excitement and fear
Between life
And death.

—from the Silver Spray cabin log

{Afterword}

THE WINTER OF 2003, during which this book was written, was a devastating avalanche season in western Canada. Twenty-eight people died, including two skiers at the Slocan Chief cabin. RCMP officer Terry Barter and his dog, Bela, were called out to assist with the searches for twenty-two of those victims. "It was not a pretty year," Barter says, summing up.

Snow conditions in 2003 were similar to those of 1998, except that this time the snowpack was treacherous right through to spring. It was another El Niño year, with a dry start to the winter. Faceted layers developed within the shallow snowpack early in the season. It was a year that kept staff at the Canadian Avalanche Centre on edge, anticipating the next disaster and its accompanying media storm.

"We need to understand that occasionally we will have these worst-case-scenario years," said Evan Manners as the season wound to a close. In the wake of the numerous accidents, many people called for more frequent public bulletins, but Manners points out that dispensing information is not enough: "What you really need is a population that's well-enough educated to make the best use of the bulletins." Manners felt that many people heading into the backcountry in 2003 did not understand the risks. "It hadn't got through to them that this was a year when normal behavior just wasn't going to cut it," he said. CAC bulletins encouraged skiers to scale back their ambitions with phrases such as, "The mountains are not going anywhere and there are many more winters yet to come." But many skiers still didn't get it, and a record number paid with their lives.

Canada usually has about sixteen avalanche fatalities a year. The United States averages around twenty-six. (Colorado leads the statistics, followed by Alaska, Utah and Montana.) European countries such as Switzerland, France and Austria, which have a much higher density of skiing activity per square kilometer of backcountry, each experience twenty to thirty avalanche-related deaths annually. Of course, those figures pale beside the staggering death toll in countries such as Peru, Afghanistan, Tajikistan, Turkey or Pakistan, where slides spill onto unprotected roads and demolish villages. All the same, the dramatically rising trend in North American fatalities is worrisome.

One consequence of a bad avalanche year is that fiscal purse strings loosen. After the horrendous 1999 avalanche season in Europe, governments there put money into drastically improving their nations' avalanche safety activities. Evan Manners hopes the same thing will happen in Canada, since despite the worldwide reputation of Canadian programs and expertise, the country is now at the bottom of the heap when it comes to per capita funding on avalanche safety, compared with other countries that market themselves as winter recreation destinations. "We're barely able to put out the bulletin half the time, let alone teach people the best way to use it," Manners admits.

Like everyone in the avalanche community, avalanche expert Dave Smith was troubled by the 2003 statistics. "It was a terrible season for avalanche fatalities, and many of us in the industry felt like we failed to reach people with good information and advice," he said, looking back. Smith points to a couple of key areas where he believes backcountry travelers are making big mistakes.

The first is in their choice of terrain. "I always advise my students to be as conservative as possible," Smith says. "That's the best defense you have of minimizing your exposure to risk." If skiers aren't choosing safe terrain, he explains, they are relying on their assessment of the snow stability to keep themselves safe. "And that's not a good place to go, because nobody's very good at that. There are 'bomber' days when you can feel pretty good about the snow and get away with a lot of exposed terrain. But other times the subtleties of the snowpack can escape you entirely. The more you have to rely on snow stability assessment to keep you safe, the more likely you are to make an error."

The second area where Smith believes backcountry skiers need to get smarter is in their awareness of group dynamics. "Dialogue with each other, talk things over before you commit to a slope," Smith urges. "Sometimes even people with fifteen or twenty years of experience will go out and not say a word to each other, subduing their own intuitions and deferring to each other to a fault."

222

The mountains teach tough lessons. In his book *Staying Alive in Avalanche Terrain,* Utah Avalanche Center's Bruce Tremper writes, "The pros survive by learning to master their arrogance and nurture their humbleness." Generally, we gain wisdom through experience and through making mistakes. But when you err in an avalanche zone, it might be the last error you ever make. Like Icarus, you may discover that you've flown too close to the sun.

There are dangers everywhere in life, however, and those who sweat their way up the slopes to swoop down through untracked powder are passionate about exploring life's possibilities. On many winter days in the West Kootenays, the valleys fill up with thick cloud. High above that fog is a glorious landscape bathed in sunlight, where snow crystals sparkle and white-blanketed peaks glisten. Those in the valley bottoms are having yet another dreary gray day, but up here in the mountains it's heaven. On days like that, there's no finer place to be.

{Further Reading}

*

WEBSITES

www.avalanche.ca (Canadian Avalanche Centre,
including public avalanche bulletins and a list of
recreational avalanche course providers).

www.avalanche.org (links to regional avalanche centers
throughout North America as well as the AAA and the
USFS National Avalanche Center).

www.csac.org (Cyberspace Snow and Avalanche Center).

MANUALS

Tony Daffern. *Avalanche Safety for Skiers, Climbers and
Snowboarders.* Rocky Mountain Books, rev. ed. 1999.

Jill Fredston and Doug Fesler. *Snow Sense: A Guide to
Evaluating Snow Avalanche Hazard.* 2001.

Bruce Jamieson. *Backcountry Avalanche Awareness,* 7th ed.
Canadian Avalanche Association, 1989, rev. 2000.

Bruce Jamieson and Jennie McDonald. *Freeriding in Avalanche Terrain: A Snowboarder's Handbook*. Canadian Avalanche Association.

Bruce Jamieson and Darcy Svederus. *Sledding in Avalanche Terrain: Reducing the Risk*. Canadian Avalanche Association.

David McClung and Peter Schaerer. *The Avalanche Handbook*. The Mountaineers, 1993.

Bruce Tremper. *Staying Alive in Avalanche Terrain*. The Mountaineers Books, 2001.

MAGAZINES

Couloir Magazine. www.couloirmag.com.

{Acknowledgments}

T O TELL THE STORY of this avalanche, I needed the generous cooperation of dozens of people. Families, friends, searchers and others who were personally affected by the tragedy took a leap of faith when they agreed to talk to me. It can't have been an easy decision to allow a stranger to shine a public light onto a private tragedy, but many did this in the belief that others can learn from what happened. I am tremendously grateful for their trust, and I hope that, as they read this book, they will feel that trust was well placed. Some people chose not to be interviewed or to provide input for the book; I understand their reservations and respect their right to privacy.

I could not have written this book without the acquiescence of Carrie Fitzsimons; I thank her for that courageous decision. My appreciation goes to other family members for their openness: Carleen and Gordon Leidal, Vince Nicola, Yvette Stolth, Jacqueline Casano, Bob Bradley, Lori Byrd and

Greg Jewett. My appreciation also to the skiers' friends and colleagues, including Bruce Fairley, Angelina Eisele, Alice Weber, Monica Nissen, Deb Zeeben, Wren McElroy, Greg Stone, Scott Belsey, Gerry Chatelaine and Johnny Smoke, who contributed their recollections and stories. Among the many others who provided information about this avalanche and related matters (and I can't possibly list them all), particular thanks to Dave Smith, Tom Van Alstine, Marc Deschenes, John Buffery, Sean McTague, Cathy Grierson, Dave Heagy, Kevin Giles, Andy Tyers, Murray Springman, Tim Rippel, Terry Jones, Cal Lloyd, Karl Denboer, Anna Reid, Shannon Hames, the RCMP's Jay Arnold, Terry Barter and Bruce McLellan, helicopter pilots Duncan Wassick and Keith Westfall, and Coroner Shawn Jestley. For a broader perspective on avalanche issues, I turned to Evan Manners from the Canadian Avalanche Centre, Mark Mueller of the American Avalanche Association, Bruce Jamieson, Juerg Schweizer and Peter Hoeller. Andrej Arajs, Dale Caton, Maureen Jansma and Jeff Gfroerer provided details of other avalanche incidents in the area. Brian Moulson, Jan Flett and Roland Perrin explained medical and critical-incident debriefing procedures; reporters Bob Hall and Ian Mulgrew related their experiences covering the accident; Ron Lakeman provided meteorological expertise; Steve Flett filled me in on backcountry recreation issues in the region; and Dr. Gerald Wilde helped me understand the psychology of risk.

Much of the technical information on avalanches was gleaned from manuals written by North American snow scientists and avalanche educators, including Bruce Tremper, Bruce Jamieson, David McClung, Peter Schaerer, Tony Daffern, Doug Fesler and Jill Fredston. I'm indebted to these professionals for their valuable information born of years of experience. I've attempted to credit their input where appropriate, but apologize in advance if there are any instances where their words or phrases are echoed in this manuscript without sufficient acknowledgment. It's the kind of slip-up that can happen in the midst of a mammoth research effort.

The British Columbia Arts Council provided financial assistance for the writing of this book. Laurie Pollard transcribed dozens of interview tapes, and Holley Rubinsky provided initial editorial advice. The final shape of this book owes much to the fine editing of Barbara Pulling. Her sound judgment, sure guidance and tactful suggestions helped me make it through a daunting task.

My immediate family, Eric, Guy and Joel, always remind me that there is life beyond deadlines, and make me glad to climb out of my basement office at the end of a long day. Finally, thanks to the friends with whom I have spent so many wonderful days skiing in the mountains.

{About the Author}

✳

VIVIEN BOWERS writes for a wide variety of
publications in Canada and the United States. Her books
have won numerous honors, including a Canadian
Science Writers Association Award, an Information Book
Award and the Sheila A. Egoff Prize. She lives with
her husband and two sons near Nelson, British Columbia,
where she regularly goes backcountry skiing.